D1539904

Developmental Approaches to Academic Advising

Roger B. Winston, Jr., Steven C. Ender,
Theodore K. Miller, *Editors*

NEW DIRECTIONS FOR STUDENT SERVICES

URSULA DELWORTH and GARY HANSON, *Editors-in-Chief*

Number 17, March 1982

Paperback sourcebooks in
The Jossey-Bass Higher Education Series

Jossey-Bass Inc., Publishers
San Francisco • Washington • London

Developing Approaches to Academic Advising
Number 17, March 1982
Roger B. Winston, Jr., Steven C. Ender, Theodore K. Miller, *Editors*

New Directions for Student Services Series
Ursula Delworth and Gary R. Hanson, *Editors-in-Chief*

New Directions for Student Services (publication number USPS
449-070) is published quarterly by Jossey-Bass Inc., Publishers.
Second-class postage rates paid at San Francisco, California,
and at additional mailing offices.

Correspondence:
Subscriptions, single-issue orders, change of address notices,
undelivered copies, and other correspondence should be sent to
New Directions Subscriptions, Jossey-Bass Inc., Publishers,
433 California Street, San Francisco, California 94104.

Editorial correspondence should be sent to the Editors-in-Chief,
Ursula Delworth, University Counseling Service, Iowa
Memorial Union, University of Iowa, Iowa City, Iowa 52242
or Gary R. Hanson, Office of the Dean of Students,
Student Services Building, Room 101, University of Texas
at Austin, Austin, Texas 78712.

Library of Congress Catalogue Card Number LC 81-48488
International Standard Serial Number ISSN 0164-7970
International Standard Book Number ISBN 87589-920-X

Cover art by Willi Baum
Manufactured in the United States of America

Ordering Information

The paperback sourcebooks listed below are published quarterly and can be ordered either by subscription or as single copies.

Subscriptions cost $35.00 per year for institutions, agencies, and libraries. Individuals can subscribe at the special rate of $21.00 per year *if payment is by personal check.* (Note that the full rate of $35.00 applies if payment is by institutional check, even if the subscription is designated for an individual.) Standing orders are accepted.

Single copies are available at $7.95 when payment accompanies order, and *all single-copy orders under $25.00 must include payment.* (California, Washington, D.C., New Jersey, and New York residents please include appropriate sales tax.) For billed orders, cost per copy is $7.95 plus postage and handling. (Prices subject to change without notice.)

To ensure correct and prompt delivery, all orders must give either the *name of an individual* or an *official purchase order number.* Please submit your order as follows:

Subscriptions: specify series and subscription year.
Single Copies: specify sourcebook code and issue number (such as, SS8).

Mail orders for United States and Possessions, Latin America, Canada, Japan, Australia, and New Zealand to:
Jossey-Bass Inc., Publishers
433 California Street
San Francisco, California 94104

Mail orders for all other parts of the world to:
Jossey-Bass Limited
28 Banner Street
London EC1Y 8QE

New Directions for Student Services Series
Ursula Delworth and Gary R. Hanson, *Editors-in-Chief*

Contents

Editors' Notes

During the past decade academic advising has captured the interest of both student affairs practitioners and academic faculty members, leading to national conferences and ultimately to the formation of the National Academic Advising Association. The current literature suggests that academic advising has great potential for affecting change in modern higher education. The changing population of students, the need to increase retention, the need of students for adult role models, student consumerism, and the intent of many colleges and universities to provide educational programs that reflect their mission statements of educating the whole student have generated new interest in academic advising. Concern about the academic advising process presents an opportunity for student service professionals to extend student development concepts beyond the realm of traditional cocurricular programming into the whole institution and to begin institutionalizing an integrated approach to educating students that addresses personal as well as intellectual development.

This sourcebook examines academic advising from the perspective of student development theory. The rationale for such an approach builds on the realization that the advisor's office, with its many systematic student contacts, is a powerful mechanism for implementing intentional student development. However, analysis shows that many present-day advising programs operate as bureaucratic, clerkish activities on the periphery of effective educational services. Obviously, much important work remains.

As Ender, Winston, and Miller point out in Chapter One, developmental advising cannot occur without collaboration among the institution's faculty, student affairs staff members, and academic administrators. A rationale and definition of developmental advising are given, and the roles of individuals involved in the program and the politics of the institution must be recognized and considered if there is to be an integrated academic-student affairs advising program.

In Chapter Two Miller and McCaffrey present a theoretical overview of both psychosocial and cognitive theories of human development and outline many of the major developmental tasks students face in these areas. Strategies for assisting students in their growth are highlighted for developmental advisors as well.

David Crockett presents an excellent overview of a variety of academic advising delivery systems in Chapter Three. He presents current approaches to academic advisement, factors to consider when selecting a delivery system, various types of delivery models, and essential components common to any advising system. Crockett's chapter concludes by depicting a model academic advising delivery system that incorporates a combination of delivery models.

Brown and Sanstead summarize the research literature on academic advising and discuss evaluative processes for making decisions about the advising process. They present a brief review of several evaluation approaches and identify the critical issues affectd by the academic advising process. They also present several key qualities and strategies individuals must consider as they evaluate the academic advising process.

Thomas Grites discusses the many special student populations and the unique personal characteristics and needs advising programs should address. He highlights many innovative advising approaches used throughout the country to respond to the unique needs of various special populations. Special attention is paid to advising returning adult students, scholarship athletes, academic high-risk students, and honors students. In Chapter Six, Ender and Winston present the essential skills and competencies that all advisors must possess if they are to offer truly effective academic advising. This chapter identifies eleven components of advisor training and outlines goals and outcome objectives for each component. Critical issues that must be addressed in a training program are also discussed. In conclusion, Roger Winston presents an overview of recent publications in the area of academic advising in the annotated bibliography.

Many proponents of the concept of student development stress that its implementation is meant for all students enrolled in today's colleges and universities and is, in fact, the mission of higher education. Several authors agree that the principles and theories of total student development can be implemented through, and in concert with, the academic advising process. The goal of this sourcebook is to take student development theory from the hands of the theoreticians and place it in the hands of those who deal directly with students through the advising process. The collaboration of students, faculty, student affairs staff, and administrators is essential if the goal of implementing student development through the advising process is to be realized.

Finally, we would like to thank Maggie Morris, who typed countless drafts of chapters, for her endurance and patience, and Amy Bargeron, who did much of the early library research for us.

Roger B. Winston, Jr.
Steven C. Ender
Theodore K. Miller
Editors

*In order for colleges to have a beneficial impact on
the intellectual and personality development of
students, academic and student affairs divisions must
work collaboratively; academic advising should be the
touchstone for their integrated efforts.*

Academic Advising as
Student Development

*Steven C. Ender
Roger B. Winston, Jr.
Theodore K. Miller*

From its inception at Harvard in 1636, American higher education has held
as one of its primary missions the education of the whole student: mind,
body, and soul. During the first century of higher education in America,
educating the whole person was viewed as realistic and plausible. Small
communities of students and faculty were in constant interaction; both
cognitive and affective concerns were addressed by a faculty who visualized
these concerns as their raison d'etre.

Today, total student development continues to be promoted by
writers from many points of view (Astin, 1977; Bowen, 1977; Brown, 1972;
Chickering, 1969; Chickering and associates, 1981; Heath, 1968; Miller and
Prince, 1976). The same ideas are also found in almost all present-day
college catalogues. Colleges, at least implicitly, promise students, their
parents, and the general public that the education they provide is concerned with more than intellectual development (Brown, 1980a; Cross,
1980). However, most colleges today provide lip service at best to the
concept of total student development. Few colleges in the country have
consciously undertaken the systematic, sustained effort required to offer

R. Winston, S. Ender, T. Miller (Eds.). *New Directions for Student Services: Developmental
Approaches to Academic Advising*, no. 17. San Francisco: Jossey-Bass, March 1982.

total student development programs (Cross, 1980). The concern shown for student development by planning boards and other overall policy bodies, in other than the intellectual and academic area, has been largely piecemeal, haphazard, and perfunctory. As Brown (1980b) indicates, student development in a holistic sense on most college campuses is incidental and accidental. This is a sad commentary on modern higher education and antithetical to the principles upon which it was founded.

Many changes, both evolutionary and revolutionary, have caused colleges over the years to adopt a dualistic approach to the education of students (Blimling, 1981). These changes include secularization of colleges, increased enrollments, the German-inspired intellectualistic approach to education, increased specialization, emphasis on research, and the industry-bred concept of the forty-hour week (Tinsley, 1955). As a result of these changes, higher education has increasingly become compartmentalized and has "all but abandoned responsibility for moral, ethical, or emotional development in favor of admission standards based on cognitive preparation, and almost a nineteenth-century German view that faculty have no responsibility for the affective development of the student" (Blimling, 1981, p. 2). This compartmentalized, dualistic approach in higher education has resulted in the faculty addressing students' intellectual, cognitive concerns and the student affairs staff taking the responsibility for the many "nonintellectual" growth concerns of the student population.

We take strong exception to the dualistic approach to educating the whole person and believe that the integration of personality and intellectual development is an essential and viable goal of higher education. Further, we contend that such an integrated approach not only is possible, but that its touchstone is the academic advising process. This potentially potent process can be actualized through a unified effort on the part of faculty members, students, student affairs staff members, and other institutional administrators.

The advising process on most campuses presently represents one of the few educational experiences involving a one-to-one relationship with an institutional representative that all students are required to share. This existing structure provides an area in which intentional, developmental processes may directly affect most students on today's college campus. The academic advising process requires redefinition and considerable attention from institutional leaders if it is truly to promote the development of the whole student or, as referred to herein, become developmental academic advising.

A Rationale for Developmental Advising

The rationale for developmental advising is based on the fact that higher education must respond to a public trust to educate the whole student, that changes in the student population demand developmental advising, and that the research literature substantiates the positive impact of academic advising.

Higher education must respond to its public trust to educate the whole student (Blimling, 1981; Bowen, 1977; Sanford, 1979). However, graduates of higher education continue to be overrepresented among citizens who are divorced, who have mental health problems, who commit suicide, who are alcoholics, and who are white-collar criminals (Blimling, 1981). How could development of the whole student, as so many college mission statements purport to address, result in such alarming statistics? Clearly, institutions of higher education are failing. To be worthy of the public's trust, they must renew their efforts to educate the whole student in systematic, purposeful ways.

Another justification for developmental advising is that changes in the college student population have focused more attention on the need for careful systematic planning. The "new student" in higher education (Cross, 1974), characterized as a white, lower-middle-class, first-generation college student who placed academically in the bottom one-third of his or her high school class, enters college with many academic and career concerns requiring immediate attention. These students need someone to help them with their programs of study, career exploration, and personal concerns if either academic or personal success is to be achieved. The academic advisor may be one of the best and most natural persons to fill this important role for students.

Another noticeable change in student populations concerns the returning student twenty-five years of age and older. As Brodzinski (1980) indicates, this group of students has grown steadily—in 1978 one third of all students enrolled in higher education were over twenty-five. They bring their own unique problems and needs, including a certain type of consumerism, to campus. They want and *expect* support, guidance, and an educational experience highlighted with quality. The academic advisor has great potential for aiding these returning students in both taking advantage of the available resources and completing appropriate programs of study. These older students experience different academic, vocational, and personal concerns than many eighteen- to twenty-three-year-olds (Chickering and Havighurst, 1981), but their needs require intentional support, stimulation, and challenge, as do the needs of their younger counterparts.

Additional support for intentional student development through the advising process can be found in research. Several researchers (Astin, 1977; Bowen, 1977; Heath, 1968) have found significant relationships between student satisfaction with the institution and their relationship with its faculty. Satisfied students often point to the availability of personal relationships with faculty as a key factor. These findings support the fact that caring relationships with members of the academic community are extremely important to students and that they need and benefit from such relationships. A caring, supportive mentor and role model is a necessity for a quality developmental advising program, and not just one more good service.

Student retention is another factor that provides support for a developmental advising program. There has recently been a decline in the traditional-age student population. If we wish students to complete their programs of study, we must create an environment that is challenging, supportive, and caring. The academic advising program grounded in developmental theory and programming concepts can be a key ingredient to a growth-engendering climate and instrumental in influencing students to continue enrollment.

In many instances, the academic advisor is the only individual the students are obligated to visit three or four times each academic year. These visits will necessitate more than merely signing registration forms if educating whole persons capable of surviving and successfully coping with a complex world is a goal. If a primary thrust of academic advising is not the intentional stimulation of growth and development, then on many campuses chance factors will become the mode. The attitude reflected in statements such as "don't worry, if it is important, they will learn it" is the antithesis of intentional student development. Higher education must be concerned with all aspects of development—cognitive, affective, and physical alike. Students must be helped to realize the interdependence of all and the fact that the whole is truly greater than the sum of its parts. The integration of the whole can begin in the advisor's office through a deliberate program calling on the resources of the total college community. This collaboration can and should result in developmental academic advising.

A Redefinition of Academic Advising

Does the intentional education of the whole student begin with the advising process? The answer is probably a resounding "NO" if many of the current advising systems are examined. In many such programs the advisor's major role "is to keep records of students' progress toward their degree and to make sure that students have fulfilled both college and major requirements" (Walsh, 1979, p. 446). Unfortunately, this is the definition that many advising programs exemplify. For them, a redefinition of "advising" must take place if the academic advising process is ever to address the developmental needs of the whole student.

Several authorities contend that academic advising must be redefined by emphasizing students' developmental concerns (Crockett, 1978; Crookston, 1972; Grites, 1979; Mash, 1978; McCaffrey and Miller, 1980; Walsh, 1979). These authors have redefined academic advising as a decision-making process facilitated by communication and information exchange with the advisor (Grites, 1979); as the integration of academic goals with other life goals (Walsh, 1979); as the development of student goals consistent with interests, aptitudes, strengths, and background experiences (Mash, 1978); and as a teaching function whereby the advisor assists students in using rational processes, environmental and interpersonal interactions, behavior awareness, and evaluation skills (Crookston, 1972). The academic advising process can also provide students with a significant and trusted guide or consultant who assists them in articulating their purpose and life direction (McCaffrey and Miller, 1980). Crockett (1978) describes the developmental advising process as the coordination of the student's entire educational experience. Such coordination activities may include clarifying values, providing information about educational options, and monitoring and evaluating their educational progress.

As one examines the many definitions of developmental advising presented by these authors, several key conditions emerge. The following list of characteristics concerning developmental advising lays a foundation for operationally defining this process.

Developmental advising is a process, not a one-step, paper-endorsing activity. It is continuous and is established on the basis of the advisor-advisee relationship. Developmental advising is an accumulation of personal contacts between advisor and advisee. It has direction and purpose.

Developmental advising is concerned with human growth. Cognitive, affective, career, physical, and moral growth are all important components of developmental advising. Total student development recognizes that all these areas are legitimate and that personal goals and objectives are important to individual students.

Developmental advising is goal related and its goals are central to its purpose. Goals are collaboratively established and need to be owned by the advisee. Goals are established so as to provide direction for academic, career, and personal growth planning.

Developmental advising requires establishment of a caring human relationship. A personal relationship between advisor and advisee is essential to developmental advising. Both parties must take responsibility for sustaining the relationship, but the advisor must take primary responsibility for its initial establishment.

Advisors serve as adult role models and mentors. Academic advisors must understand and wisely use the personal power granted to them in the advisor role. The advisor reflects, for the student, both the image of a faculty/staff member and the philosophy of the institution. Impressions, both positive and negative, have substantial impact on students' thoughts and feelings concerning their relationship with both the institution and its personnel.

Developmental advising is the cornerstone of collaboration between academic and student affairs. The integration of faculty and student development personnel is paramount to the success of a developmental advising program. Academic advising offers a vehicle to bring the expertise and resources of both faculty and student affairs staff members to full impact on the student.

Developmental advising utilizes all campus and community resources. Advisors serve as the hub of students' learning experiences. Although advisors are not expected to possess expertise in all areas of student growth and development, they should be aware of the many human and programmatic resources available on and off the college campus.

For our purposes, the following operational definition is offered. "Developmental advising both stimulates and supports students in their quest for an enriched quality of life; it is a systematic process based on a close student-advisor relationship intended to aid students in achieving educational and personal goals through the utilization of the full range of instiututional and community resources." It is a critical higher education function that requires the involvement and expertise of both academic faculty and student affairs professionals.

Developmental advising relationships are life goal and personal growth oriented and intentionally reflect the mission of total student development by facilitating the essential processes of challenge and response or differentiation and integration as postulated by Sanford (1967) and Chickering (1969). The quality of educational life reflected in most post–secondary educational institutions is directly proportional to how effectively the academic advising program can affect the full development of the students involved.

Advisor Responsibilities

If developmental advising is to become a reality on college campuses, the individuals serving as advisors have responsibility to participate actively in its creation and maintenance. This participation has implications for relationships between both advisors and students and advisors and their institutions. The quality and outcomes of these relationships have a direct bearing on the quality of the developmental advising program.

Responsibilities to the Institution. Institutions should expect, even insist, that developmental advisors (1) assist in the formulation of the missions, goals, and objectives of the program; (2) participate in advisor training programs; and (3) seek out and implement developmental tools and strategies appropriate to the advising process.

Academic advisors must challenge the institution to articulate the mission, goals, and objectives of the advising program. Those assigned the task of advising need to hear advising's role in the educational mission clearly articulated within the college. Hopefully, advisors will take part in the creation of their own developmental advising roles and job descriptions, for few will provide the energy and time demanded if their influence is not felt on the nature and responsibilities of the role. It is extremely important that all constituencies of the college community understand and support the important position that developmental advisors play in accomplishing the educational missions of the institution. These mission statements should go beyond describing what the advising program does and begin to address what qualities and characteristics they are trying to develop in students. If advisors do not understand the student outcomes the institution is attempting to achieve through the advising process, they will have no standard by which to evaluate their advising skills or their impact on student-advisees.

Academic advisors must participate in training the institution offers to impact developmental advising. Hopefully, academic advisors possess the desire to continue their own learning and value the need to expand their academic advising knowledge and skill. Without participation in training programs designed to enhance developmental advising skills, most faculty and staff will be unable to be truly responsive to the developmental needs of their student-advisees.

In effect, without quality training programs, developmental advising will seldom if ever occur. Faculty members can bring their knowledge and expertise about the curriculum, academic requirements, and policies; student affairs professionals can do the same in the areas of human/student growth and development, career exploration, communication skills, and goal setting, assessment, and referral techniques. This knowledge and skill can be utilized in collaborative advisor development and in-service education programming. Such programs, when implemented through a collaborative team approach utilizing the skills and expertise of all educators on campus, can greatly enhance the viability of the advising program.

Relationships with Students. "When entering freshmen are asked what they think will be the dominant influence on their future life, they suggest the academic side of campus life . . . asked four years later, as seniors . . . they will describe a personality change that was influenced by an interpersonal relationship" (Brown, 1972, p. 31). Students still need and, in fact, want a mature guiding influence during their college years. The academic advisor must realize the tremendous significance the advising relationship can have for students. "Youth are socialized or identify with the adult role and move toward taking a full adult role by modeling their behavior after others perceived to be in that role" (Kramer and Gardner, 1977, p. 14). Other, older students also are seeking models. Being models for students to emulate requires a special commitment from advisors. To be successful, they must communicate their interest in students beyond talking about academic course requirements, however. Students may put up barriers to self-exploration, feeling they are taking up advisors' valuable time by introducing topics that go beyond "legitimate" academic advising. Advisors must demonstrate willingness to address other concerns and may want to reflect Chickering's (1969) admonition that helpful advisors listen, watch, feel, inquire, and respect their student-advisees.

One of the developmental advisor's major roles is to serve as the hub in the student's total learning experience (Crockett, 1978). Referring students to appropriate resources is an essential aspect of developmental advising, and advisors must be acutely aware of the available services and their relationship to student needs. Larger campuses and urban communities will have many support services and staff for students to use, but smaller campuses and communities may have more limited resources. In either instance, however, the developmental advisor will often be the first line of referral for students.

Collaboration Among Community Members

Even though it is highly desirable that all educators on the college campus who serve in administrative, faculty, and student affairs staff positions should become personally involved in the academic advising process—that is, actually serve as developmental advisors for students—a commitment to collaboration among these groups in designing the program must precede implementation. During this design phase of developmental advising, administrators, faculty, student affairs staff members, and students have specific roles and responsibilities to ensure success of such a program.

Administrators. College administrators must establish both the philosophy and objectives of the academic advising program and support its maintenance. They must be aware of the important relationships between student satisfaction, student retention, and the process of academic advising. They must come to grips with the realities that many, if not most, advising programs are not working and are highlighted by student dissatisfaction (Bostaph and Moore, 1980). Likewise, they need to understand that quality academic advising is not inexpensive in either time or money.

A true commitment to developmental advising begins with the top echelons of the college's administrative staff. This means collaboration and commitment from the president, academic vice-president, student affairs vice-president, academic deans, and departmental chairpersons. The most telling commitment an administrator can make is money. Funding a liaison position representing both academic affairs and student affairs to coordinate and plan the academic advising program would be a serious commitment to the process of developmental advising. Responsibilities of the individual in this liaison position would include coordinating the planning of the program, as well as its goals and objectives, training faculty and staff to work as developmental advisors, and evaluating the impact of the program with students, faculty, and staff participants.

It is important that the institution's leaders value the process of developmental advising. They must communicate their commitment for quality advising to faculty, staff, and students. Additionally, administrators must back up this commitment with incentives and reward systems for advisors. Without top-level administrative commitment, the academic advising program will at best be lackluster and will probably falter or fail.

Faculty. Faculty members have, and continue to be, the primary movers in academic advising delivery systems. Carstensen (1979) reports that 79 percent of all advising programs are currently maintained by the faculty. Faculty have a tremendous influence on students, as Astin's (1977, p. 223) longitudinal study of student development found. "Student-faculty interaction has a stronger relationship to student satisfaction with the college experience than any other involvement variable or, indeed, any other student or institutional characteristic. Students who interact frequently with faculty are more satisfied with all aspects of their institutional experience, including student friendships, variety of courses, intellectual environment, and even administration of the institution. Finding ways to encourage greater personal contact between faculty and students might increase students' satisfaction with their college experiences."

Faculty members serving as developmental academic advisors represent an excellent method to maintain greater personal contact with students. They must first recognize their great potential for influencing students' affective as well as cognitive growth. Their ability to be role models for students is paramount to the success of the developmental advising process. Faculty members serving in advising roles must perceive this function as much more than simply endorsing class schedules. Rather, they must begin to review the literature of student development, meet and initiate dialogue with the student development educators on their campuses, and discuss the goals of the developmental academic advising program and their participation in it.

Student Affairs Staff Members. Many student affairs professionals are experts in the area of college student growth and development. As with faculty members and administrators, student affairs practitioners cannot achieve the institution's mission alone, but must seek collaboration.

Student affairs staff members may assume several specific roles in both the development and maintenance of developmental advising programs. They may serve as advisors. To accomplish this task successfully, however, student affairs professionals must gain a knowledge and understanding of the basic academic requirements and policies of the institution.

Student affairs professionals must draw on the expertise of faculty members. Just as faculty can learn much about human relations and student development from the student affairs professional, so the reverse is true. A symbiotic relationship between student affairs advisors and faculty advisors is essential for a quality developmental academic advising program to exist.

Student Involvement. To expect developmental advising to occur because of a commitment from faculty, student affairs staff, and college administrators is not a true picture of reality. A major characteristic of the developmental advising process is the relationship between students and advisors. Students must understand how developmental advising works for them and how they can take advantage of this unique relationship with an advisor. This educational process begins with the institution admission information and bulletins relating the institutional mission to the developmental advising process. Admissions counselors must communicate to students the college's intentions to provide advisors who will challenge the student to consider their strengths and weaknesses; establish personal, academic, and career goals; utilize the many campus and community resources in goal accomplishment; learn and apply successful study skills and time management techniques; and become personally involved with their academic advisees as people. The institution must articulate the purpose of the relationship and challenge students to participate actively in the process.

A Continuing Effort. Academic affairs and student affairs must continue to collaborate even after a unified, coordinated developmental advising approach has been implemented. The student affairs division must be responsible for keeping all advisors informed about available resources and communicating any program changes or modifications on a timely basis. Likewise, the academic affairs leadership must do the same regarding its programmatic and support service resources. It would, in fact, be desirable to have someone associated with the advising program monitor all available and appropriate student referral resources. A campus and community student resources clearinghouse would be a valuable addition on most campuses.

Student Affairs Taking the Initiative

If developmental advising is to become a reality, student affairs divisions must take the initiative in bringing about change. This cannot be unilateral or exclusionary in approach. As Brown (1972, 1980b) and Miller and Prince (1976) have argued, successful implementation of the concepts of student development require collaboration among all the various institutional constituencies—faculty members, students, support personnel, and administrators. Academic advising is an ideal focal point for collaborative efforts for student development. However, an appreciation of the political realities and campus dynamics is necessary in order to effect meaningful change on behalf of students.

Politics. Institutional politics are the mechanisms by which things get done on a campus (Barr and Keating, 1979). The study of institutional politics can be thought of as constructing a topographical map of the policy-making and service delivery processes on a campus: One needs to identify the mountain ranges it may be impossible to climb, the flat plains that offer few obstacles as far as the eye can see, and the lush river valleys that may invite confrontations. To ignore the political realities of a college campus is like trying to drive cross country without paying attention to where one is going; behavior in both instances greatly increases the probability of never reaching the desired destination. Academic advising may be hidden in the clouds at the top of a mountain almost impossible to reach, on the open plain available for the taking, or in a river valley already viewed as belonging to someone else. It is critical that the political atmosphere be assessed on each campus.

Important features and landmarks to be entered on a campus map include (1) organizational norms; (2) faculty characteristics and perceptions; (3) reward systems; (4) student characteristics, wants, and perceptions; and (5) the institution's response to change (Shaffer, 1980).

Organizational Norms. Most college organizations are structured to emphasize the self-actualization of faculty and administrators rather than the education of students, a state of "negotiated normalcy," so to speak. By this we mean that rules specifying the fair and proper means for competing for resources, creating and deleting programs, and delineating spheres of influence are negotiated. Student affairs has traditionally been in a weak bargaining position in this process because many have seen its function as ancillary or peripheral (Shaffer, 1980).

Organizational norms may be looked at from three different perspectives: authority, power, and territory (Barr and Keating, 1979). Authority refers to the formal processes and personnel for making decisions within the institution. An understanding of the organizational chart, as well as an acquaintance with "critical" administrative assistants, associate directors, and secretaries, can help one determine how to present ideas and also when to be bold and when to hold back. Power in an organization has no direct correspondence to the formal structure; it is a property of individuals and can be most frequently observed by watching who influences decisions, especially across formal lines of authority. Issues regarding authority and power generally are manifested in terms of territory (the legitimate domain for exercising authority).

For student affairs to enter the arena of academic advising on many campuses means to confront issues of authority, power, and territory. Traditionally, academic advising has formally fallen under the purview of "academic affairs" and the faculty. Even if there is agreement at the higher administrative levels, such as that of vice-president, the college dean or department chairperson may well see student affairs' involvement in advising as an invasion of sacred (though often unwanted) territory. Winning the support of academic department chairpersons may be the most critical factor in establishing an effective advising program (Kramer and Gardner, 1978). They have the power to determine who is to be involved, what rewards will be made available for participation, and how formal decision-making bodies will treat advising.

Faculty Characteristics and Perceptions. As Shaffer (1980, pp. 305–306) has noted, "the socialization of professors on many campuses tends to discourage involvement in . . . activities" such as developmental advising. Younger faculty members who might have the interest are discouraged because they lack role models in this area (when they were students nor as faculty), the skills needed to be effective, and the appropriate rewards, especially when related to promotion and tenure. Older faculty members, who may possess more security within the institution, are also unlikely to seek such experience after a lifetime of lecturing, writing, and doing research.

In order for student affairs to win over a sufficient number of faculty members to make an advising program effective, we must demonstrate tangible benefits for them. Barr and Keating (1979) suggest beginning small when establishing new programs (within a small college, division, or department), soliciting faculty input, and selling in the currency of the realm (for example, personal satisfaction through meaningful student-faculty relationships, student retention if enrollments are falling, release time from teaching responsibilities, or opportunities to demonstrate competence for moving into academic administration). It is important to legitimatize student affairs' involvement in advising by creating positive images with the faculty through competent management, sensitivity to feelings, and a sound theoretical conceptualization. Whoever attempts to sell these ideas to faculty members needs to possess the credentials that faculty members respect, such as an earned doctorate, a scholarly reputation, or identification with an academic discipline.

Reward System. If developmental advising is to get a toehold, all involved need to be rewarded for making it work. If professional advisors are used, traditional incentives such as recognition, autonomy, pay, and encouragement are necessary. Involved faculty members and student affairs staff should also be rewarded through whatever means available, such as release time, summer employment, letters of commendation, merit pay increases, and recognition in promotion criteria. To expect an advising system to run without investments of money, personnel, and facilities is to predetermine failure.

Student Characteristics. Before embarking on a campaign to create developmental academic advising programs, there must be a good data base to assess student body characteristics, student needs and wants, and prevailing stereotypes or perceptions of the college environment in general and academic advising in particular. Because the characteristics of each student body makes it unique, an academic advising program must be structured to reflect that uniqueness. Strategies for dealing with the special concerns of various subpopulations of students (see Chapter Five) must fit into the overall system to assure that all segments of the population are served and to minimize conflicting purposes and wasted resources within the advising system.

Responsiveness to Change. Most higher education institutions are reactive or resistant to change "because those who hold the most potential to alter an organization are precisely those who may lose the most if the system is changed" (Borland, 1980, p. 221). Many in the institution view student affairs' primary role as maintainer of the status quo, that is, keep the students in line, keep the hallways outside class quiet, and thwart extremes in fads and life-styles (Shaffer, 1980). It therefore may appear incongruent in the eyes of many for student affairs staff members to be the movers for change within the institution.

If student affairs is to make an impact on the advising system, a number of antecedent conditions need to exist. The student affairs division must build an image on campus of an organization composed of professionals who possess an area of expertise. Alliances with important decision makers and holders of power need to be built on other issues (the best way to get a favor is to give one). Personal relationships of trust need to be established with academic administrators who influence decisions about academic advising. Finally, do not go empty-handed. If the student affairs division wishes to have influence and input into the advising process, it must be willing to contribute the necessary resources, such as money, part-time staff, space, or support services. Advice on how to do it, though the expertise be great, is unlikely to be favorably received by academic administrators.

Summary

This chapter has articulated the important relationship between academic advising and the intentional personal development of college students. We have emphasized the importance of an integrated academic advising approach, which calls for collaboration between and among all segments of the campus community and seeks to provide joint ownership to all involved. Each institution must create its own unique response to the important area of advising students, but a number of essential elements deserve special attention in any program of academic advisement. The remaining chapters focus attention upon these important considerations.

16

References

Astin, A. W. *Four Critical Years: Effects of College on Beliefs, Attitudes, and Knowledge.* San Francisco: Jossey-Bass, 1977.

Barr, M. J., and Keating, L. A. "No Program Is an Island." In M. J. Barr and L. A. Keating (Eds.), *New Directions in Student Services: Establishing Effective Programs,* no. 7. San Francisco: Jossey-Bass, 1979.

Blimling, G. S. "Residence Halls in Today's Compartmentalized University." In G. S. Blimling and J. H. Schuh (Eds.), *New Directions for Student Services: Increasing the Educational Role of Residence Halls,* no. 13. San Francisco: Jossey-Bass, 1981.

Borland, D. T. "Organization Development: A Professional Imperative." In D. G. Creamer (Ed.), *Student Development in Higher Education: Theories, Practices and Future Directions.* Washington, D.C.: American College Personnel Association, 1980.

Bostaph, C., and Moore, M. "Training Academic Advisors: A Developmental Strategy." *Journal of College Student Personnel,* 1980, *21,* 45-50.

Bowen, H. R. *Investment in Learning: The Individual and Social Value of American Higher Education.* San Francisco: Jossey-Bass, 1977.

Brodzinski, F. R. "Adult Learners—The New Majority: A Demographic Reality." In A. Shriberg (Ed.), *New Directions in Student Services: Providing Student Services for the Adult Learner,* no. 11. San Francisco: Jossey-Bass, 1980.

Brown, R. D. *Student Development in Tomorrow's Higher Education: A Return to the Academy.* Washington, D.C.: American College Personnel Association, 1972.

Brown, R. D. "Developmental Transcript Mentoring: A Total Approach to Integrating Student Development in the Academy." In D. G. Creamer (Ed.), *Student Development in Higher Education: Theories, Practices, and Future Directions.* Washington, D.C.: American College Personnel Association, 1980a.

Brown, R. D. "The Student Development Educator Role." In U. Delworth and G. R. Hanson and Associates, *Student Services: A Handbook for the Profession.* San Francisco: Jossey-Bass, 1980b.

Carstensen, D. J. *A National Survey of Academic Advising.* Iowa City, Iowa: American College Testing Program, 1979.

Chickering, A. W. *Education and Identity.* San Francisco: Jossey-Bass, 1969.

Chickering, A. W., and Associates. *The Modern American College: Responding to the New Realities of Diverse Students and a Changing Society.* San Francisco: Jossey-Bass, 1981.

Chickering, A. W., and Havighurst, R. J. "The Life Cycle." In A. W. Chickering and Associates, *The Modern American College: Responding to the New Realities of Diverse Students and a Changing Society.* San Francisco: Jossey-Bass, 1981.

Crockett, D. S. "Academic Advising: A Cornerstone of Student Retention." In L. Noel (Ed.), *New Directions for Student Services: Reducing the Dropout Rate,* no. 3. San Francisco: Jossey-Bass, 1978.

Crookston, B. B. "A Developmental View of Academic Advising as Teaching." *Journal of College Student Personnel,* 1972, *13,* 12-17.

Cross, K. P. *Beyond the Open Door: New Students to Higher Education.* San Francisco: Jossey-Bass, 1974.

Cross, K. P. "Education for Personal Development." In D. A. DeCoster and P. Mable (Eds.), *Personal Education and Community Development in College Residence Halls.* Washington, D.C.: American College Personnel Association, 1980.

17

Grites, T. J. *Academic Advising: Getting Us Through the Eighties.* Washington, D.C.: AAHE-ERIC Higher Education Research Report, no. 7, 1979.

Heath, D. H. *Growing up in College.* San Francisco: Jossey-Bass, 1968.

Karmer, H. C., and Gardner, R. E. *Advising by Faculty.* Washington, D.C.: National Education Association, 1977.

Kramer, H. C., and Gardner, R. E. "Managing Faculty Advising." In D. S. Crockett (Ed.), *Academic Advising: A Resource Document.* Iowa City, Iowa: American College Testing Program, 1978.

McCaffrey, S. S., and Miller, T. K. "Mentoring: An Approach to Academic Advising." In F. B. Newton and K. L. Ender (Eds.), *Student Development Practices: Strategies for Making a Difference.* Springfield, Ill.: Charles C. Thomas, 1980.

Mash, D. J. "Academic Advising: Too Often Taken for Granted." *The College Board Review,* 1978, *107,* 32–36.

Miller, T. K., and Prince, J. S. *The Future of Student Affairs: A Guide to Student Development for Tomorrow's Higher Education.* San Francisco: Jossey-Bass, 1976.

Sanford, N. "Developmental Status of the Entering Freshman." In N. Sanford (Ed.), *The American College: A Psychological and Social Interpretation of the Higher Learning.* New York: Wiley, 1967.

Sanford, N. "Student Development and the American College." In N. Sanford and J. Axelrod (Eds.), *College and Character.* Berkeley, Calif.: Montaigne, 1979.

Shaffer, R. H. "Analyzing Institutional Constraints upon Student Development Activities." In D. G. Creamer (Ed.), *Student Development in Higher Education: Theories, Practices and Future Directions.* Washington, D.C.: American College Personnel Association, 1980.

Tinsley, M. A. "The Faculty Advisor in the Liberal Arts College." *Personnel and Guidance Journal,* 1955, *34,* 219.

Walsh, E. M. "Revitalizing Academic Advisement." *Personnel and Guidance Journal,* 1979, *57,* 446–449.

Steven C. Ender is assistant professor in the student personnel in higher education program in the Department of Counseling and Human Development Services at the University of Georgia. He has served as an academic advisor for developmental studies students for three years and has extensive consulting experience training faculty, staff, and students in the acquisition of helping skills.

Roger B. Winston, Jr., is assistant professor in the student personnel in higher education program and director of the Student Development Laboratory at the University of Georgia's Department of Counseling and Human Development Services. While an associate dean of students, he served as coordinator of an experimental freshman-year advising program.

Theodore K. Miller is professor of education and coordinator of the student personnel in higher education program in the Department of Counseling and Human Development Services at the University of Georgia. He is chairperson of the University of Georgia's faculty advisory board to the division of developmental studies, a program designed for high academic risk students.

Effective advising programs can be
founded on theories of human development,
which can guide advisors as they seek to create
environments conducive to students' educational
and personal growth.

Student Development Theory: Foundations for Academic Advising

Theodore K. Miller
Sue Saunders McCaffrey

If academic advising is to focus on the totality of the student's interaction with the higher education milieu, knowledge of human development theory and an understanding of the potential influential factors implicit in a college or university are necessary. This chapter examines the relationship of both human development and environmental interaction theories to academic advising programs and their implications for the development of academic advising principles.

The academic advisement process, which reflects one of the most important aspects of the higher education experience for students, is too often based upon the rather simplistic idea that students need help deciding upon which academic courses to take. Although these are important considerations, there are many others that a high-quality advising program seeks to reflect, for both educational and personal factors are involved. Ideally, academic advisement focuses attention upon the totality of students' interaction with the higher education enterprise, not simply upon their course of study or institutional requirements.

R. Winston, S. Ender, T. Miller (Eds.). *New Directions for Student Services: Developmental Approaches to Academic Advising*, no. 17. San Francisco: Jossey-Bass, March 1982.

The Rationale for Academic Advising

To be most effective, academic advising must be founded upon a sound theoretical rationale. One of the most appropriate, if education is designed to foster student growth and change, is developmental theory. From this perspective, the student is viewed as a dynamic entity who is associated with an institution designed to stimulate and guide people toward more advanced levels of knowledge, competence, skill, and personal well-being. In other words, students seek out the higher education experience to become more fully developed human beings who possess the capacity to deal with life in ways that will better assure them the quality of life to which they aspire. Many students may not be able to articulate clearly why they seek higher education, but, for most, self-enhancement, self-reliance, and self-direction are important. To be responsive to these life goals, the academic advisement program must consider the total student, not just some unrelated aspects of the student, as its primary mission. Education does not take place in a vacuum, and neither does the development of human beings. Because the interaction between the individual and the environment is so important to human development, it appears sound to found the academic advising program firmly upon developmental theory. This decision, however, has many implications for those involved in implementing the program, as well as for those who will benefit from it.

An academic advisement plan based upon developmental theory calls for an understanding of and belief in certain basic assumptions that underlie the theory. There are several different clusters or families of formal developmental theory from which to choose (Knefelkamp, Widick, and Parker, 1978; Rodgers, 1980; Rodgers and Widick, 1980). For our purposes the psychosocial development theories of Havighurst (1953, 1972), Erikson (1968), and Chickering (1969) and the intellectual development theories of Piaget (1952), Kohlberg (1969), and Perry (1970) are emphasized. These two theoretical families represent different but complementary ways of conceptualizing human development. The psychosocial development theories focus primary attention on the content and behavioral characteristics of development; the intellectual development theories emphasize processes of development, particularly in terms of the way individuals think and learn. Blending the psychosocial and intellectual theories and combining the developmental principles upon which they are founded enables us to arrive at a sound rationale for implementing an academic advising program designed to deal directly with students' developmental needs. If these development principles are emphasized within their organizational structures, the advising programs will more completely model the theories upon which they are based.

Developmental Principles. Some developmental principles common to most human beings have been identified and are helpful in aiding our understanding of the developmental processes experienced. First, human development is continuous in nature. It begins at conception and continues throughout life. Although not a straight line process, for it has many peaks, valleys, and plateaus, development continues no matter what one's age or environment.

Second, human development is cumulative in nature. One's history becomes the foundation for future growth and change. What has occurred influences subsequent development. Different people have different experiences and thus are at different developmental levels and have different developmental needs. The concept of individual differences is much in evidence. Therefore, it should not be assumed that there is one best resolution to similar developmental situations for all people.

Third, human development follows a simple to complex continuum. All development begins at a simpler, less complex level and grows toward the more complex. As Sanford (1967, p. 47) says, *"development means, most essentially, the organization of increasing complexity."* As one continues to grow and change, one accumulates new experiences and learnings that are additive. One thereby grows more mature and able to function more successfully at higher levels of abstraction and complexity.

In addition, human development tends to be orderly and stage related. Most authorities have concluded that many developmental characteristics are relatively common to us all and that development seems to progress in an organized series of stages. For both families of theories, stages are important and are viewed as being sequential in that they tend to occur in a certain order. Intellectual theorists tend to view developmental stages as being sequentially invariant, universal, hierarchical in nature; and they are concerned primarily with the process development takes, not the content. Psychosocial theorists tend to see developmental stages as sequential, but not essentially invariant, not necessarily universal in nature, and not structurally hierarchical. The psychosocial theorists are concerned with the *content* of development more than with the detailed processes involved. Both families view stages as qualitatively different from each other in the sense that the process and/or content changes for each stage. The psychosocial developmental theorists tend to see the "recycling" of content issues and tasks as being quite common; whereas the cognitive developmental theorists do not view the process experiences encountered by individuals as ever being ordinarily "re-experienced" once they have been initially encountered.

Developmental Model of Academic Advising. A developmental model of academic advisement would have at least four characteristics not typically found in most institutions' programs. First, it would be based upon the developmental principles previously noted and would seek to assimilate and synthesize these elements into a comprehensive whole. Both intellectual and personal-emotional aspects of development would be of primary concern. The present developmental status or level of the individual student would be kept in focus, and each student would be aided in understanding the way human development unfolds, how it comes about, and what it usually involves. Only as students are educated about the process as well as the content of their own development can the advising program truly become developmental as defined in Chapter One and as reflected in the writings of Crookston (1972), Chickering (1973), and Walsh (1979), among others. Second, a developmental model of academic advisement would incorporate systematic training. For developmental advisement to become a reality, highly qualified and competent individuals must take responsibility for the program.

Those directly responsible for the advising process are obviously important to the success of the program, yet there are many others peripherally involved. Both the faculty and academic administrators responsible for specific educational programs, even if they do not directly perform academic advising functions, must be recognized as important to the developmental advising program. They must believe that the developmental advising program is viable, desirable, and responsible. In light of this important factor, the third characteristic of a developmental model for academic advising would include the establishment of an academic community support group, including faculty and academic administrators not directly involved in the academic advising processes.

A fourth characteristic of a developmental model of academic advisement is based on the principle that human development occurs through cycles of differentiation and integration. The motivation for development results from the discovery that one's earlier learnings or behaviors are simpler than the new awareness or the comprehension that more complex concepts, actions, or interests are involved. The cyclical aspect of this process is evident as the individual moves to ever-increasing levels of complexity as a result of having discovered earlier differentiations and responding to their challenge by first assimilating and then integrating the new with the old.

As previously noted, there is reason to believe that life's challenges and responses to them are important to the development of people of all ages. College students, whether youthful or mature in years, are particularly susceptible to developmental pressures because they have associated themselves with an educational environment designed to promote growth and change. Developmental advisement programs, then, may well be established with the intent of using existing life challenges or conflicts as a basis for facilitating the developmental processes experienced by those served. By possessing a relatively accurate understanding of the developmental tasks to be faced and the developmental processes to be experienced by students at all ages, the developmental advisor can better help in creating an environment to achieve the tasks and/or experiencing the process essential to students' development. Likewise, the better developmental advisors can structure their interaction with students around identified developmental themes those students experience, the more likely these interactions are to stimulate and promote total student development.

Environmental Influences. Most individuals agree with the premise that the higher education experience influences not only one's educational development but also the eventual course of one's intrapersonal, interpersonal, career, educational, and physical development. However, the precise nature of the interaction between individual and environmental influences has not been finally determined.

Certain characteristics of the educational environment facilitate the positive development of students in the personal, social, career, educational, and physical domains. The advising program should be a key variable in creating an environment that fosters this development. Drawing upon theories of organizational development, social learning, and developmental psychology, one can paint a picture of an ideal environment purposefully designed to foster sufficient developmental opportunities for both traditional and nontraditional college students. A developmental environment is one in which there is

- A balance between stimulation and support
- Congruity between individual needs and environmental characteristics
- A sense of common purpose shared by various college operations
- Encouragement to develop meaningful relationships with peers
- A variety of opportunities to make meaningful decisions and to control one's destiny
- A provision for effective role models and significant relationships with faculty and staff members.

To encourage students' development, academic advisors should help create educational environments that provide enough support to allow students to take risks but not so much that they become complacent and resist change. Such an environment would satisfy individual needs to the point that students feel comfortable in confronting the challenges of the educational environment. Another way academic advisors can help students grow and develop is to make sure that they create educational environments in which the institutional goals and values are readily apparent through the practices, services, and educational methodologies in that institution. For an environment to be truly developmental, the advisor should provide opportunities for students to meet and interact with others who share interests, concerns, and values. Students also grow when they have the opportunity to make decisions about their future, to explore values, and to develop effective problem-solving skills. The academic advisor may help students choose among courses, majors, instructors, values, friendships, and careers. On a college campus, effective faculty role models have a significant impact on student development. Academic advisors can either serve as role models or put students in touch with other faculty who are willing to disclose their values, beliefs, successes, and failures and show by personal example how to cope with major life decisions. In short, academic advisors can serve as mentors for students (McCaffrey and Miller, 1980).

Application Strategies. A well-organized, systematic, and orchestrated developmental advising approach, based upon both cognitive and psychosocial human development theory and integrated throughout the academic environment, is the most viable alternative if total student development is the goal. The more one realizes and acts on the fact that advising programs are only as good as (1) the theory upon which they are based, (2) the systematic procedures and environmental resources used, and (3) the qualifications and competencies of those who implement them, the greater the likelihood of success. These three factors notwithstanding, the key to successful operationalization of a developmental academic advising approach continues to be the leadership's ability to marshall institutional resources into an integrated program that is collaboratively created and carried out.

In effect, a successful strategy or model for a developmental academic advising program must (1) be relatively comprehensive in nature, (2) take into account the overall mission of the institution, (3) incorporate principles of human development and learning, (4) seek to utilize the total institutional environment, and (5) be responsive to the developmental and educational needs of individual students within the academic community. Although each individual student is ultimately responsible for his or her own personal, educational, and social development, the institution has the primary responsibility to make the necessary resources available to all students. These resources include the advisement program, for this is practically the only activity all students experience on a continuing basis throughout their college years. To act on this knowledge by creating an environment that uses advising processes as its core makes good sense and is strongly recommended.

There is no formula, recipe, or cookbook available to create a single model for use on a given campus. Each institution must look to both the theory and its own unique characteristics and needs and be prepared to create approaches designed to meet its students' needs within the prevailing institutional context. What follows is an attempt to outline the marriage of two families of developmental theory, psychosocial and cognitive, in a comprehensive advising program.

SPICE. A framework including both psychosocial and physical developmental concerns for academic advising can be derived from the research literature and current student development practice. Such a framework can identify several key themes of personal development upon which an advising program can focus. The central or core theme for such a configuration would be the self, paying particular attention to students' intrapersonal development. How one perceives oneself indicates how one perceives the world. Individuals also possess a physical being. Because human existence requires maintenance of that physical self, this also becomes an important part of such a thematic framework. In addition, human beings cannot exist entirely alone, for social needs are paramount. Therefore, the interpersonal aspects of human development would also be included as an essential part of such a developmental advising structure. In similar fashion, the vocational or career aspects of life are important, for the vast majority of college students are especially concerned with this. Finally, a common psychosocial developmental theme for all college students relates to the academic or educational. This area of concern reflects both the reasons for becoming a student and the processes by which a student's goals are to be achieved. Formulation of this thematic framework of advising establishes that the *self,* the *physical,* the *interpersonal,* the *career,* and the *educational* are all essential aspects of human development and must therefore be considered as important to any developmental advising program. By blending these five areas, a framework referred to as the *SPICE of Developmental Life* can be created: a simple play on words, but not a simple approach.

One of the primary purposes of higher education is to influence the direction that life takes. Chickering and Associates (1981, p. 10) express this clearly: "every college and university, public or private, church related or not, is in the business of shaping human lives. They will continue to be. It is one of the fundamental reasons for their existence. It is the bedrock basis for state support, federal incentives, and tax-exempt status."

If the shaping of human lives is the essence of higher education, then both the process and the direction of that shaping is important and should be reflected in the framework of the academic advising program. The thematic components of the SPICE of Developmental Life framework reflect the developmental content derived from human development theory, which the advising can directly impact. The developmental tasks, for instance, which can readily be identified within each of the five components, make excellent guides for programmatic response to students' personal developmental needs. The advising activities that reflect that response then become an important part of the process by which students' lives are shaped. Examples of advising response options for some of the developmental tasks reflected in the SPICE of Developmental Life framework for different developmental stages are presented in Table 1.

The Perry Scheme. Creating an environment in which both students' personal and intellectual developmental needs are addressed in an integrated fashion is no easy task, but it is one which all advisors should attempt. Applying cognitive development theory to practice within the context of academic advising does call for a clear understanding of how

Table 1. Sampling of Adult Life Cycle Tasks and Developmental Advisement Program Responses

STAGE	SPICE Component	Tasks	Example Advising Response
Late Adolescent and Early Adult Transition Years Ages 16-23	Self	1. Emotional independence	1. Dealing with authority figures or discovering responsible assertions
		2. Instrumental autonomy	2. Building creative problem-solving skills or discuss academic major option
		3. Develop an ethical system	3. Activities to resolve moral/ethical dilemmas by discussing academic honesty
	Physical	4. Meet biological needs	4. Human sexuality and contraception seminars or discuss personal hygiene
		5. Increase manual skills	5. Athletic and sports activities
		6. Advance recreational skills	6. Explore lifelong fitness and nutrition activities
	Interpersonal	7. Freeing interpersonal relations	7. Human relations training or discussion of social activities' options
		8. Develop capacity for mature intimacy	8. Building intimate relations skills by discussing dating practices
		9. Increase tolerance	9. Cultural differences simulation or discuss alternative values
	Career	10. Identify interests	10. Vocational interest assessments and discussing likes and dislikes
		11. Assess abilities	11. Aptitude and skill assessments or discuss success experiences
		12. Choose a career	12. Career planning and decision-making consultations
	Educational	13. Identify and use educational resources	13. Study skills assessment and study improvement sessions
		14. Make mature educational plans	14. Educational alternatives seminars and discuss educational options
		15. Select appropriate academic major	15. Analyze various academic disciplines
Early and Young Adulthood Years Ages 23-35	Self	1. Developing integrity	1. Values clarification workshops
		2. Achieve personal identity	2. Self-exploration and discussing life purpose alternatives
		3. Establish interdependence	3. Group participation skill building by discussing mutuality, dependence, and independence
	Physical	4. Consume wisely	4. Consumer-budget management or discuss time management options
		5. Identify leisure interests	5. Recreational activities guidance
		6. Manage stress	6. Relaxation response training and discuss test-taking

	Developmental Tasks	Possible Programmatic Responses
	8. Expand peer relationships	8. Overcoming shyness by discussing social outlets and skills
	9. Assume civic responsibilities	9. Campus action projects or refer to community social programs
Career	10. Start an occupation	10. "How to succeed" workshops and discuss part-time work options
	11. Establish career directions	11. Employment realities discussions
	12. Handle career demands	12. Dealing with world of work by discussing work ethics and expectations
Educational	13. Identify continuing educational needs	13. Life purpose clarification by discussing long-term educational alternatives
	14. Adjust to continuing education	14. Continuing education orientation
	15. Revise educational plans	15. Reassess life purpose by discussing alternative educational plans
Mid-life Transition and Middle Adulthood Years Ages 35-57		
Self	1. Reexamine personal values	1. Values clarification & goal setting or reassessment discussions
	2. Search for meaning	2. Discuss personal life-style values and ethics
	3. Adapt to changing time perspective	3. Long-term management by life planning discussions
Physical	4. Identify appropriate physical outlets	4. Alternative activities discovery by discussing fitness options
	5. Increase health consciousness	5. Health maintenance discussions and wellness programs
	6. Manage stress effectively	6. Stress and anxiety management by discussing life pressures and handling increased demands
Interpersonal	7. Reassess life-style	7. Discuss intimacy in relationships and commitments to others
	8. Relate to maturing children	8. Discuss changing relations and communication patterns
	9. Relate to aging parents	9. Dealing with aging and death by discussing responsibilities for older parents
Career	10. Reassess career objectives	10. Adult life-purpose discussions through reexamination of interests and needs
	11. Progress up career ladder	11. Discuss advanced success strategies or examine ethical & life-style contradictions
	12. Revise career plans	12. Discuss mid-life career alternatives and coping with career changes
Educational	13. Reassess educational plans	13. Re-entry student advising groups or discuss alternative learning resources
	14. Increase likelihood for academic success	14. Sharpen study skills by discussing current approaches and strategies
	15. Relating to younger teachers & students	15. Discuss conflict avoidance and how to obtain support from peers

students think, view the world of ideas, and change their views as they encounter new experiences. One theoretical construct that has excellent utility for academic advising is the Perry (1970, 1981) scheme. The blending of the SPICE of Developmental Life framework with the Perry scheme represents a viable integration of cognitive and psychosocial developmental theories as a sound rationale for a developmental academic advising approach.

As with most helping interactions, the advisor must understand the student's current developmental position and respond to individual students so as to recognize their unique needs, and create enough dissonance to challenge their present way of thinking. An advisor who provides too many challenges or who forces a student to operate at advanced levels of functioning too quickly can contribute to overstimulation and thus can inadvertently thwart developmental progress.

Integrating Perry and SPICE

The remainder of this chapter focuses on the integration of the Perry theory of intellectual development with the SPICE framework and provides examples of how advisors might respond to students in different positions.

The Perry scheme of intellectual and ethical development represents a continuum divided into a nine-position sequence that can be clustered into four categories. This scheme outlines the evolution of college students' thinking processes about the nature of knowledge, truth, and values and the way people make meaning out of their experiences along the way. For the academic advisor, the four categories—dualism (positions 1–2), multiplicity (positions 3–4), relativism (positions 5–6), and commitment (positions 7–9)—have utility for better understanding the intellectual processes involved in the ways different students visualize the world. Some descriptive examples will be helpful in understanding the ways such thought patterns influence students' lives and therefore the advising process.

Dualism. Students in positions 1–2 tend to view the world in absolutes. Something is either true or it is untrue; it is either good or it is bad; it is either right or wrong. Correct answers are thought to exist somewhere for every problem, and they are thought to be known by the authorities. Similarly, the locus of life control is usually viewed as being largely external to oneself. Psychosocially, students in these positions may have particular difficulty in dealing with others who do not or are not willing to tell them what is right or how to do something in particular. Their tolerance for other viewpoints and life-styles may be rather low and their willingness to examine alternative responses very limited. Although they may have an identified academic major, they may well not be able to give any specific reasons for selecting it or they may have picked it because a parent or a respected adult authority said it was right for them. Career and educational plans are likely to be viewed as things not directly under the student's control and probably in the hands of the college authorities.

Students at these levels of cognitive development might well seek out the authority of their teachers and advisors. An academic advisor, therefore, is seen as a person who should know the right answers and who will tell the student what is required in order to succeed. The advisor is viewed as being in control, and although he or she may sometimes ask questions or present problems, the student believes this is being done so as to make the student discover the "right answer" for him or herself. For students who think dualistically, the advisor is a powerful and important person who is viewed as possessing knowledge. Likewise, the student who is probably in awe of such a powerful person will not usually seek out extra and unrequested interactions with the advisor. The dualistic level student will probably not view an open invitation to "drop by and talk" as a real invitation.

For students in the dualism position, the common student concern with the selection of academic courses will likely be translated into an expectation that the advisor tell them what courses to take. Characteristics of an example student that indicate he or she is currently in a dualism position might include (1) the need for the advisor to determine "correct" course selection, (2) the student's feeling that he or she does not have ultimate control over educational plans, or (3) the lack of a clearly defined rationale for course selection or choice of major. This student would also be unlikely to visualize the advisor's role as that of a mentor or resource for personal development. Instead, the advisor is seen as an authority whose sole responsibility involves short-term educational planning and giving specific answers and advice. If advisors wish to assist such students in moving to a more advanced position, they should resist the temptation to provide students with a quick and easy answer.

The advisor should attempt to help the student identify alternatives and choose among them. Perhaps, initially, the advisor may even suggest two or three alternatives and ask the student to identify one course alternative to examine more closely. The advisor and student could then generate both advantages and disadvantages of that and the other alternatives. In this fashion, the advisor assists the student to move from a dualistic to a multiplistic position while tailoring responses to the student's present level of readiness.

Multiplicity. Students who view the world from multiplicity positions admit that not all the correct answers are currently known and that, therefore, there is some legitimate place for different opinions and maybe even values. As a result of this growing awareness, students in the multiplicity positions often conclude that because no one knows for sure, any opinion must be acceptable and none can be considered as being truly "wrong." Even so students often believe that if they persist long and hard they may yet be given the "right" answers by someone in authority.

Students in multiplicity positions are challenged by the need to examine their own belief systems, often for the first time, as they prepare to answer existential questions such as "who am I" and "what am I to become." In many instances, they are faced with having to deal with massive amounts of new information and ideas and others' values, which have, until this time, not appeared so obvious to them.

Career and educational options begin to appear more important, and some doubts about past plans may arise. Personal aptitudes and interests may be coming into conflict with experiences in college; so increased levels of insecurity and self-doubt are present. In many ways, this is a time of transition from the security of knowing that the world is stable with many absolutes to guide one's relationships and activities to the insecurity of realizing that things are not as simple as they used to seem, that people are asking for "reasons" to support what is believed or said or done, and that friends are expecting new and different things from their relationships. Occasionally, students will respond to these new awarenesses by seeking to deny their existence. They may delay the growth by dropping out or retreating into dualistic processes that reflect denial or rejection of others' views. They may even evidence dislike or outright hatred for others who are different.

For the advisor, this means that students (1) may be open to considering suggestions about some of the apparently new alternatives available to them or (2) may possibly react to them with denial or outright rejection of such new possibilities. Some students may yet believe there is a right answer somewhere and may pressure the advisor for the answer. Or they may reject the advisor's thinking because they suspect he or she doesn't really know any more about it than they or others do; so no one can actually say they are wrong about what to do, or what course to take, or in which activities to participate. Likewise, because peer influence is strong, students may view the advisor's opinions as being in the minority and therefore less acceptable—or less desirable—than others.

Advisors may discover that students in multiplicity positions are difficult to work with and may even be inclined to seek ways to limit interaction with them. No matter how difficult it is for the advisor personally, however, students in these positions can benefit considerably from the kinds of serious interaction and questioning the advisor can provide. For many students, this is the first time they have been able to think on their own, and they may not yet have learned to do it well.

Career and educational planning issues are important for most college students, but particularly for those students who view the world in a multiplistic fashion. These issues can become disconcerting and fraught with confusion. Take, for example, the sophomore student who had "always" planned to be a veterinarian but is not doing well in the basic sciences. The student has not thought about other career options and has limited awareness of his skills, talents, aptitudes, and interests. Frequently, this student may seek the "right" answer from numerous sources and expect that answer to provide an appropriate career alternative. The student may shift majors frequently or may vehemently reject all suggested career alternatives.

Characteristics indicating this student is struggling with multiplistic positions include (1) the need to examine his long-range career plans, perhaps for the first time, (2) the need to assimilate information about performance in the basic sciences that threatens an important self-perception, and (3) the need to encounter constructively feelings of insecurity and doubt. This student is likely to view the advisor with ambivalence. On the one hand, the advisor may be an important source of new information. On the other hand, that information may exacerbate feelings of insecurity and doubt. Although advanced development occurs as a result of challenge and response, some students may seek to avoid some of the challenges presented them.

The advisor in this situation would need to respond to the student's feelings of insecurity and may need to help the student develop strategies for constructively communicating confusion to parents and peers.

Because career planning is such a common concern for students, the advisor may wish to organize several students into a career/academic major decision-making group. In this way, students can share ideas and come to realize that confusion about careers is by no means a unique phenomenon. One goal of these group sessions would be to teach students ways to gather career information from a wide variety of sources. Also, students should be instructed how to devise personally relevant criteria to evaluate such information. By this process, students can move toward a relativistic position in which the source of information is considered important and opinions are evaluated in terms of personal needs, values, and abilities.

Relativism. Students who reason relativistically give much greater weight to the source of the opinion or solution than do students at the lower position levels. The quality of the knowledge is seriously considered and viewed in relation to the context in which it is experienced. Comparative analyses are sought, and students usually seek to determine where and how things fit together into a more integrated whole. Authorities are less likely to be resisted, although the locus of control is increasingly internalized, moving the student ever closer to becoming the self-directed learner and person so essential to survival in an increasingly complex society. Also, in the advanced levels of these positions, students realize they must individually come to grips with the relativistic world in which they live and make some personal decisions about which stands to take and which values to hold.

Students in the relativism positions become increasingly aware of the impact of their environments upon their lives. It is clear by now that there is a vast diversity of opinion available to them, and they are discovering that it is increasingly important for them to make personal decisions about what is best depending upon the context in which it exists. This means that individual students are focusing more attention upon who they are in light of their educational and social environment. For nontraditional students, this may be especially problematic because their diverse backgrounds, when compared with higher education environments, may result in great conflict. Such differences deserve special attention.

Likewise, this is particularly a time when personal values are being examined and tested in light of new relationships involving levels of intimacy beyond being friends or acquaintances. Awareness that one's survival depends upon establishing interdependence with others, and that authorities may be valued for their expertise in guiding and aiding rather than for providing answers, begins to grow as well. Concern for the larger community and awareness that one has varying amounts of responsibility for others as well as oneself also is emerging at this time. Leisure activities may begin to shift toward community service orientations and away from purely self-interest areas for some. Most students are also reexamining their career decisions in light of these new awarenesses.

In close proximity to these discoveries is the awareness that one's education is increasingly one's own responsibility and that no one can truly teach another but can only facilitate learning. An implicit danger here is that as the importance of taking personal responsibility for one's life grows, some students seek to avoid the accompanying tension or anxiety by seeking to escape by abandoning responsibility by rejecting society's expectations for such behavior on the part of its adult members. It is also important to realize that students in relativism positions are moving increasingly closer to being more fully mature and self-directed learners who may expect different things from their educational experiences than institutional leaders have anticipated. As a result, students at this point may seek to change the institution and its curricular and cocurricular offerings in various ways. In effect, as students discover new ways of making meaning from their experiences, they may actually seek to alter the environment that has nourished these new awarenesses. Over the years, students have often brought about campus change; such changes may be directly attributable to the advanced thinking processes associated with the positions of relativism.

For academic advisors, this means that students in these positions have different needs now than they did previously. Because there are so many alternatives and they are all relative, the student's responsibility is to decide which is best depending upon the context of the situation, hopefully with some guidance from an advisor who will help in the evaluation process and give honest, concerned feedback. Students at this level need more than simple answers and advice; they need consultation and opportunity both to identify and to test out the alternatives open to them.

An example of an effective relationship between a student in relativism and an advisor is the female student who is attempting to balance needs for an intimate family relationship with needs for a highly successful career path. The student is struggling with mature life-style considerations and ways to meet personal needs and ideals. The student in this situation is able to identify alternatives clearly and to evaluate consequences of each. Also, this student sees these choices as her responsibility and is seeking to find a feasible balance among alternatives that is consistent with her values. Flexibility and openness to new ideas characterize a student in these realistic positions.

Characteristics of this student that indicate she is involved with positions in relativism include (1) taking personal responsibility for life-style choices, (2) the need to anticipate the impact of work and family environments on personal need structure, (3) the desire to gather opinions from a wide variety of sources, and (4) the need to test the reality of her career decisions in light of personally identified life-style needs. This student is likely to see the advisor as one who possesses a valued opinion and can give feedback on the feasibility of alternatives. This student is more likely to view the advisor as a mentor than are students in positions of dualism or multiplicity.

The advisor's role in this situation is to listen, question, and suggest. Ideally, the advisor would assist the student in drawing upon available resources for additional evaluation of possible alternative plans. It may be helpful for the student to talk with peers or older adults who have tentatively resolved similar life-style questions. Perhaps the student could arrange to participate in a women's group whose members have career responsibilities as well as family concerns. In addition, the student might wish to provide tutoring for returning women, thereby establishing interdependent relationships with older women. If possible, the student could spend time or even live with a dual-career couple and, ultimately, be enabled to see the many nuances of such a life-style.

This type of intervention could establish for the student a supportive environment that provides a variety of role models. In addition, by providing the student with the opportunity to develop a comprehensive future-focused image, the student's movement toward commitment positions is enhanced.

Commitment in Relativism. Students who have reached the most advanced positions of the Perry scheme are involved in making personal commitments based upon their awareness of relativism. These advanced positions are less concerned with the structure of the learning process and more concerned with the process of identity development through the purposeful selection and affirmation of views and beliefs closely aligned to one's life purpose. Allport (1962, p. 378) reflected upon the "remarkable ability of human beings to blend a tentative outlook with firm commitment to chosen values" and quoted the poet Tennyson: "there lives more faith in honest doubt, believe me, than in half the creeds" to highlight this unique characteristic. In the Perry scheme, the advanced positions represent emerging and evolving commitments made in the full awareness that the responsibility for them is internalized by the student and that new learnings may alter these beliefs and commitments even more. Reflecting upon how students at the most advanced position see the world, Perry (1981, p. 79) writes, "this is how life will be. I must be wholehearted while tentative, fight for my values yet respect others, believe my deepest values right yet be ready to learn. I see that I shall be retracing this whole journey over and over—but, I hope, more wisely."

Psychosocially, students in the advanced positions of commitment in relativism have "made an active affirmation of themselves and their responsibilities in a pluralistic world, establishing their identities in the process" (King, 1978, p. 39). This means that students at these levels have largely internalized the locus of control and generally function on relatively autonomous levels in relation to parents, teachers, administrators, advisors, and peers. They do, however, tend to seek additional opportunities to expand their horizons and their awareness about the world about them. Many people at this level have established well-balanced leisure-work relationships or are seeking to do so. They are probably becoming more health conscious and may be involved in "wellness" activities that will become an integral part of their adult lives. Interpersonally, they are making commitments toward life-styles and possibly even toward life partners at this time. At the very least, they are beginning the process of making choices that will directly influence the remainders of their lives. Commitments toward careers and specific long-range educational plans are being decided upon, and, in many instances, a reassessment of life purpose is also being initiated. Basically, students at the advanced positions of commitment in relativism are concerned more with moral, ethical, and identity development than with the intellectual development so apparent in the earlier positions. At this point, students need consultation and help in identifying and utilizing campus and community resources more than direct guidance or advisement as such. They perceive the importance of their own responsibilities in relation to their world and will seek to act upon these perceptions if given the freedom to do so.

This is the time students need the support of someone who believes they can and will be able to handle such important processes as making commitments in the full awareness that the world is a relative place, which may well mean that some of those commitments will be altered sometime in the future. Students at this level of intellectual and ethical development need consultation and dialogue with other adults who have been faced with some of the same difficult decisions and who have both made personal commitments and survived them with dignity.

In all likelihood, not many young adult college students will reach the commitment positions during their initial higher education experience. With the increased enrollments of older students, however, more advisors may be encountering students dealing with the commitment positions. The advisor's role for students in commitment involves being a sounding board and being a person who shares their values, ethical decisions, and struggles toward integrity.

The adult who is attempting to redefine the purpose of his or her career in terms of personal identity may effectively serve as an example of these commitment positions. This sample adult student is returning to college to develop a new, more challenging career. Yet this student, although he or she has clear purposes for college attendance, still needs consultation from a significant other. Characteristics that indicate this student is involved with commitment positions include (1) a clearly defined rationale for college attendance, (2) an openness to examining various alternatives while maintaining confidence in one's ability to make an effective, personally owned decision, and (3) the need to reassess one's life goals and purposes.

The advisor may be able to facilitate development by sharing personal experience, fears, hopes, and dreams. Yet the advisor in this situation should maintain a relationship of mature interdependence with mutual give and take. Students in the commitment in relativism positions realize the importance of making their commitments, tentative as they may be, on the basis of an individual decision. The advisor's role with these people increasingly becomes one of being a mentor and colleague within the framework of an adult-to-adult relationship.

Summary

This chapter has identified several of the key developmental principles that underlie both intellectual and psychosocial development. Academic advisors should consider both of these theoretical families as they seek to create health-engendering environments so important to developing college students. The nature of these environments has also been examined in an attempt to focus attention on the ways theory can more directly influence practice in the academic advising arena.

In particular, we have tried to identify specific examples of ways that both psychosocial developmental content and cognitive developmental process can be integrated so that intentional developmental academic advising programs can be created. Combining psychosocial with intellectual development theory gives the academic advisor a comprehensive framework upon which to base the advising approach. Both life-coping skills and intellectual and ethical development are considered important components of the advising process. Present attempts to create and implement academic advising programs based upon human development theory are in their infancy, but with diligent effort, those responsible for the academic advising programs can create increasingly effective developmental approaches for their work with college students.

References

Allport, G. W. "Psychological Models for Guidance." *Harvard Educational Review*, 1962, *32*, 373–381.

Chickering, A. W. *Education and Identity*. San Francisco: Jossey-Bass, 1969.

Chickering, A. W. "College Advising for the 1970s." In J. Katz (Ed.), *New Directions for Higher Education: Services for Students*, no. 3. San Francisco: Jossey-Bass, 1973.

Chickering, A. W., and Associates. *The Modern American College: Responding to the New Realities of Diverse Students and a Changing Society*. San Francisco: Jossey-Bass, 1981.

Crookston, B. B. "A Developmental View of Academic Advising as Teaching." *Journal of College Student Personnel*, 1972, *13*, 12–17.

Erikson, E. H. *Identity: Youth and Crisis*. New York: Norton, 1968.

Havighurst, R. J. *Human Development and Education*. New York: Longman, 1953.

Havighurst, R. J. *Developmental Tasks and Education*. (3rd ed.) New York: McKay, 1972.

King, P. M. "William Perry's Theory of Intellectual and Ethical Development." In L. Knefelkamp, C. Widick, and C. A. Parker (Eds.), *New Directions for Student Services: Applying New Developmental Findings*, no. 4. San Francisco: Jossey-Bass, 1978.

Knefelkamp, L., Widick, C., and Parker, C. A. (Eds.). *New Directions for Student Services: Applying New Developmental Findings*, no. 4. San Francisco: Jossey-Bass, 1978.

Kohlberg, L. *Stage and Sequence: The Cognitive-Developmental Approach to Socialization Theory and Research*. New York: Rand McNally, 1969.

McCaffrey, S. S., and Miller, T. K. "Mentoring: An Approach to Academic Advising." In F. B. Newton and K. L. Ender (Eds.), *Student Development Practices: Strategies for Making a Difference*. Springfield, Ill.: Thomas, 1980.

Perry, W. G., Jr. *Intellectual and Ethical Development in the College Years*. New York: Holt, Rinehart and Winston, 1970.

Perry, W. G., Jr. "Cognitive and Ethical Growth: The Making of Meaning." In A. W. Chickering and Associates, *The Modern American College: Responding to the New Realities of Diverse Students and a Changing Society*. San Francisco: Jossey-Bass, 1981.

Piaget, J. *The Origins of Intelligence in Children*. New York: International Universities Press, 1952.

Rodgers, R. F. "Theories Underlying Student Development." In D. G. Creamer (Ed.), *Student Development in Higher Education: Theories, Practices and Future Directions*. Washington, D.C.: American College Personnel Association, 1980.

Rodgers, R. F., and Widick, C. "Theory of Practice: Uniting Concepts, Logic and Creativity." In F. B. Newton and K. L. Ender (Eds.), *Student Development Practices: Strategies for Making a Difference*. Springfield, Ill.: Thomas, 1980.

Sanford, N. *Where Colleges Fail.* San Francisco: Jossey-Bass, 1967.

Walsh, E. M. "Revitalizing Academic Advisement." *Personnel and Guidance Journal,* 1979, 57, 446–449.

Theodore K. Miller is professor of education in the Department of Counseling and Human Development Services in the College of Education, University of Georgia. He is also director of the Center for Student Development and coordinator of the Student Personnel in Higher Education Preparation Program.

Sue Saunders McCaffrey is currently associate director of the Division of Developmental Studies, University of Georgia. Her interests include counseling and advisement programs for high-risk students, investigation of career decision-making processes, and inquiry into nonintellective factors related to academic success.

Each institution must select the delivery system or combination of systems most appropriate for its situation and student body.

Academic Advising Delivery Systems

David S. Crockett

Academic advising, like most educational programs and services, has been delivered in a variety of ways by colleges and universities. The effectiveness of these delivery systems has varied from campus to campus. A critical evaluation and review of different delivery systems can be helpful to institutions seeking ways to modify their existing advising programs in order to make them more responsive to student needs.

This chapter discusses the various ways academic advising services are currently being provided by institutions and examines some factors to consider in selecting and organizing an appropriate and effective academic advising system. A model advising delivery system that incorporates a combination of delivery systems is presented.

Carstensen and Silberhorn (1979) reported that colleges perceive the need for identifying a model or organizational framework for the delivery of advising as one of the most important needs for their advising programs. In a similar survey, Cook (1980) found that fewer than 20 percent of the respondents rated their advisement programs excellent or outstanding. These findings suggest that many college and university personnel concerned with the improvement of advising programs are not satisfied with their present delivery mechanisms.

R. Winston, S. Ender, T. Miller (Eds.). *New Directions for Student Services: Developmental Approaches to Academic Advising*, no. 17. San Francisco: Jossey-Bass, March 1982.

There are clearly more similarities than differences in the approaches institutions take in the delivery of academic advising services. Carstensen and Silberhorn (1979) found that 75 percent of the institutions surveyed indicated faculty as the primary delivery mode for advising. Cook's (1980) study also confirmed academic advising as basically a faculty function on a majority of campuses. Despite the overwhelming use of instructional faculty for advisement, one fourth of the institutions have selected an alternate delivery system for their academic advising. Faculty advising is often supplemented by other campus personnel, such as peer advisors, professional advisors/counselors, and nonprofessional advisors. In general, however, most institutions traditionally have relied on faculty to carry out the advising function.

The most common organizational structures for the delivery of advising according to Carstensen and Silberhorn (1979) are the following:
- Entering freshmen assigned on the basis of intended major with special services for undeclared, transfers, EOP, and so on (51 percent)
- Entering freshmen assigned to selected advisors, but not necessarily on the basis of intended major (21 percent)
- Academic advising center for general advising, after which advisors are assigned by major (9 percent)
- Academic advising center for all undergraduate advising (5 percent)

No delivery system is "best" or most appropriate for all institutions of higher education. Academic advising programs must be designed to meet the specific advising needs on each campus and to reflect the unique institutional setting and situation. Therefore, the delivery of academic advising cannot be totally prescriptive.

Improvement in delivery of advising is both possible and needed if institutions are going to address adequately the changing advising needs of students in the 1980s. These modifications of existing advising delivery systems will require creativity, receptivity to new ideas, and a willingness to change the more traditional approaches to the delivery of this important service.

Selecting an Appropriate Delivery System

Prior to determining an appropriate institutional delivery system for academic advising, one must consider a number of factors that shape the ultimate design of the system. Until these topics have been thoroughly discussed, data collected and analyzed, and consensus has been reached, any decisions regarding delivery would be premature.

Advising Needs of Students. What are the advising needs of students at our institution? This fundamental question must be addressed at the outset of any discussion of possible advising delivery systems. A survey of both advisors and students should be conducted to obtain data on the possible success and the possible failure of the present program and the perceived need for change. Grites argues persuasively in Chapter Five that the advising needs of certain subgroups of students vary and delivery strategies employed need to reflect these differences.

Numerous studies of student perceptions of the advising process have been conducted (Bostaph, 1977; Chathaparampil, 1971; Cummer, 1961; Cunningham, 1975; Hardy, 1976). These and other studies reveal four major factors that students most frequently cite as important to them in the advising process. These factors are (1) accessibility, (2) specific and accurate information, (3) advice and counsel, and (4) a personal relationship with the advisor. Regardless of the delivery system selected, the institution should ensure that the system addresses these important student needs.

Organizational Structure of Institution. Clearly, the organizational structure of the institution will influence the delivery of academic advising, Cook (1980) reported that advising was directed by the chief academic officer in approximately 70 percent of the institutions surveyed, not a surprising finding given that most institutions rely heavily on faculty for the delivery of advising services. Administrative responsibility is therefore, appropriately linked to delivery. For example, should an institution decide to deliver advising primarily through counseling staff, it would be reasonable to place administrative responsibility with the chief student affairs officer. Combination delivery systems, cutting across administrative. areas of responsibility create a different type of management problem for academic advising delivery systems. As a general rule, administrative authority and responsibility should reside with the unit most directly involved in the delivery of the service. In most cases, this will be assigned to the academic side of the institution's organizational structure.

Desired Outcomes. The type of delivery system should be predicated on the desired outcomes for the advising program. A clear statement of institutional philosophy in relation to the advising program should be developed and a theoretical and functional model of academic advising should be selected. O'Banion (1972), Crookston (1972), Dameron and Wolf (1974), Grites (1977), Mash (1978), and Titley (1978) have all described advising models rooted in the belief that the advising function is a decision-making process that should facilitate student growth and development, rather than merely tending to the more prescriptive, mechanical, and course scheduling aspects of the activity. Walsh (1979) also presents a convincing case for redefining advising so that the developmental functions (that is, exploring, integrating, and synthesizing a student's academic, life, and career goals) are central to the process.

Despite this fairly recent emphasis on a developmental approach to advising, Carstensen and Silberhorn (1979) found that those responsible for the delivery of advising services still perceive the primary function to be information dissemination to students, course selection, and class scheduling. Institutions need to formulate the major objectives for the academic advising program before determining the most appropriate delivery system to realize those objectives. For example, one would organize an advising program differently if the major objective was information giving rather than assisting students to formulate sound academic and career plans.

Available Resources. A practical consideration in the design of an appropriate delivery system for advising is the amount of resources an institution is willing to allocate to the advising function. Human, fiscal, and even space resources may dictate to some extent the type of delivery system that is practical.

Ward and Higginson (1978) describe the establishment of a center for academic advisement at Murray State University in an environment where funding was low, personnel few, space small, demands high, and advisees numerous. It might, for example, be difficult to consider the establishment of a centralized advisement center in a time of fiscal constraint. However, advocates of a centralized advising system (McCauley and Fletcher, 1977, p. 14) argue, "Decentralized advising is, in the opinion of many university officials, more economical. On the surface, centralized advising would appear to be more expensive because one can easily determine the costs. In many institutions it is difficult to ascertain the costs of decentralized advising since the reduced load factor is buried in collegiate and departmental budgets. We believe the utilization of teaching faculty with reduced loads to be much more expensive." Even assuming teaching faculty are not given reduced loads, decentralized advising may also have other hidden costs (that is, secretarial assistance, lack of time to spend on other important faculty responsibilities, and so on). Pappas (1978) relates how an advisement center was created at the University of Utah by combining already existing personnel and space resources. Allocation of adequate resources is a tangible measure of administrative support and commitment to the advising function.

Collective Bargaining or Faculty Contract Agreements. If an institution is considering using faculty members in the advising delivery system, collective bargaining agreements and faculty contracts may restrict the design and implementation of the delivery system. Grites and Teague (1980) concluded that academic advising as a faculty responsibility clearly tends to be neglected in both collective bargaining agreements and faculty contracts/handbooks. If such agreements make little or no mention of advising responsibilities, efforts to improve the delivery of this important service will be more difficult for the administrator responsible for the advising program. Academic advising responsibilities must be more clearly defined and specified in future agreements.

Advisor Load. In designing an effective advising delivery system, careful thought must be given to the desired ratio of advisors to advisees. To perform effectively, advisors must be assigned a reasonable load of advisees. A delivery system that prescribes too heavy advisor loads will inevitably result in unavailability, hurried contacts, lack of personal involvement, and, in general, poor advising experiences for students.

Cook (1980) reported that the typical faculty advisor load was between one and thirty advisees. Carstensen and Silberhorn (1979) found very similar faculty advisor/advisee ratios. Advisor/advisee ratios are clearly a function of the delivery system employed by the institution. McCauley and Fletcher (1977), for instance, reported advisor/advisee ratios of one to eight hundred in a centralized universitywide advisement center using full-time professional advisors. Therefore, the type of advising delivery system selected will directly impact advisor load. Obviously, an unreasonable number of advisees, regardless of the delivery model, will weaken the quality of the advising services provided.

Delivery Models

Faculty. Institutions have relied heavily on faculty members as the major providers of academic advising services. The emergence of this predominant delivery model is easily understood from a historical perspective because student-faculty relationships have always been viewed as an integral part of the higher education process.

Faculty advising systems have emerged primarily because it has been assumed, correctly or incorrectly, that faculty members are interested in advising and consider it important. A faculty member may be the most appropriate person to guide students in course selection and the most knowledgeable individual to provide academic information to students, and this form of delivery may represent the most financially feasible way to provide the service. In considering a faculty advising delivery system, however, these assumptions should be thoroughly tested. Numerous research studies over the years have examined some of these basic assumptions regarding faculty advising. An early study on advising (Miller, 1950, p. 454) found, "While there is greater concern for the welfare of the individual college student today than was true a generation ago, indifference still characterizes the efforts of many faculty advisors." More recent studies have focused on a variety of problems associated with faculty advising: Bogard, Hornbuckle, and Mahoney (1977), Mash (1978), Grites (1979), Borland (1973), Duncan (1973), Dressel (1974), and Hallberg (1964). The potential problems with faculty advising identified by these studies can be summarized as follows:

1. Faculty advisors tend to be subject matter oriented and lack universitywide information and knowledge.

2. Faculty advisors are not generally provided with an adequate reward system for advising.
3. Not all faculty members are interested in advising or recognize the importance of this service.
4. Faculty advisors are often not as accessible as advisors in other delivery systems.
5. Faculty members lack training in the skills and techniques necessary for effective advising.
6. Faculty members have competing priorities and interests, such as teaching and research.
7. Faculty members have difficulty in keeping updated on institutional regulations, procedures, job outlooks, and so forth.

These factors must be adequately addressed if an institution is going to rely primarily on faculty for the delivery of academic advising. Given the problem areas and the many studies that have shown student dissatisfaction with faculty advising when compared directly to other delivery systems (Grites, 1979), one might easily conclude that faculty members do not represent a viable delivery mechanism for advising services.

Faculty advisors, however, are experts in their discipline and knowledgeable about specific courses in their department and in educational and career opportunities in their area of concentration. The advising process also facilitates the development of mutually beneficial relationships between student and teacher. Grites (1979, p. 13) makes an important point when he states, "One must be cautious not to generalize about the inadequacy of faculty advising. This age-old concept has yet to be shown intrinsically ineffective and should not be discarded. Rather faculty advising should be considered for its effectiveness, especially as it is coordinated with other delivery systems."

Professional Counselors. Second to faculty advising, the most frequently used advising delivery system is professional advisors. This delivery model has been particularly popular with community and junior colleges. Carstensen and Silberhorn (1979) found that approximately one third of the two-year institutions surveyed relied on professional counselors as the primary delivery system through which advising services were provided to students. These professional counselors are most often located in student counseling centers.

There are obvious advantages to the use of professional counselors as advisors. Counselors are free from academic department biases, which can plague a faculty advising system. More important, however, they have the prerequisite skills and training to be effective advisors.

The use of professional counselors as advisors also has several limitations. As pointed out by Pappas (1978) and Grites (1979), professional counselors, as a result of their training and background, are often more interested in psychological and therapeutic counseling and less interested in academic advising. Advisee load also becomes a real problem for many institutions using only counselors for academic advising. Finally, counselors find it more difficult to be as knowledgeable about specific course content, departmental requirements, graduate school opportunities, or career opportunities in specific fields as the faculty member who is a discipline expert in his or her field.

Peer. The concept of using upperclass students as "peer helpers" in orientation programs, as residence hall assistants, and as tutors has had a long tradition in higher education. In more recent years, however, institutions have turned increasingly to this group as a means of supplementing their academic advising delivery system. Carstensen and Silberhorn (1979) found that approximately one third of the institutions surveyed were using peers to support their primary mode of providing advising services. The single most persuasive argument for peer advising is that it works. The literature on this delivery mechanism strongly supports the assumption that peer advisors can be as effective as professionals and faculty in most advising situations (Baldwin, 1975; Habley, 1979a, 1979b; Murray, 1972; Upcraft, 1971; Zunker and Brown, 1966).

Peer advising can be an economical way of delivering academic advising, especially in colleges and departments with large numbers of advisees. Carstensen and Silberhorn (1979) reported that approximately 50 percent of the institutions employing peer advisors paid them. This compensation is obviously less than would have to be paid to professional staff serving a similar function.

Delworth, Sherwood, and Casaburri (1974) cite other advantages of peer advising programs, such as an awareness and empathy with common student problems in the institutional environment and freeing professional staff to deal with developmental programming, problem solving for individual students, and general advising system concerns.

Despite the obvious effectiveness of peer advising and the several advantages indicated, the use of peers, like any delivery method, has some disadvantages. About the time peer advisors gain experience and have developed their skills, they are ready to graduate. Another disadvantage is that most peers do not have the experience, background, or skill to deal with complex problems. These disadvantages, however, are not so serious that they should preclude consideration of this form of delivery. As with faculty advising programs, many potential disadvantages of peer advising can be overcome by attention to the selection, training, and management of those involved in a peer advising program.

There are some good examples of successful peer advising programs currently operating at colleges and universities. These programs can serve as useful models to institutions considering the implementation of a peer advising program. Illinois State University (Habley, 1979a), SUNY Fredonia (Looney, Anderson, and Andrews, 1978), University of Wisconsin-

Superior (Barman and Benson, 1980), University of Texas (Lagowski and Hartman, 1979), Wheaton College, Millsaps College, University of Vermont (Ellison, Kane, and Kelly, 1979), and the University of Cincinnati (Friedman, 1979) have all developed peer advising programs using a variety of methods in diversified institutional settings.

Paraprofessionals (Nonstudents). A relatively small number of institutions use paraprofessionals as adjuncts to the advising delivery system. Anyone familiar with college and university settings recognizes the valuable "informal" advising that often occurs through departmental secretaries, clerks in the registrar's office, and so forth. These systems are generally not formally recognized as delivery systems, and, often as not, individuals in these positions receive no specialized training for the advising responsibilities. King (1979), at Ocean County Community College, New Jersey, organized a more formalized program that used volunteer retired persons, housewives, and evening advisors who were employed elsewhere during the day to serve as advisors to students.

The advantages of an organized program of paraprofessional advisors would be continuity, freeing professional staff for more substantive work with students, a sense of worth and contribution by the paraprofessional, and cost. Paraprofessionals can be adequately trained to provide accurate and specific information to students on routine matters related to the advising process. Unfortunately, they do not generally possess the background, depth, and experience to deliver the full range of developmental advising services cited earlier in this chapter. However, as a supplement to other delivery systems, the use of paraprofessionals as advisors has merit.

Computer-Assisted Advising. Although more of a supplement than a replacement of other forms of delivery, computer-assisted advising has proven in several institutional settings to be an effective and efficient support service for academic advisors. Some of the specific uses of this technique include verification of graduation requirements, identification of students in academic difficulty, and provision of demographic and course information (Grites, 1979). The obvious advantage to this technique is its ability to provide current information on advisees in a timely fashion. For example, an advisor can receive a printout each quarter or semester for his or her advisees showing courses completed to date, grades earned, courses or hours needed to complete major or minor requirements, and so forth. Such a system can provide advisors relief from repetitive clerical record keeping, thus allowing the advisor more time with the advisee on the substance of the advising process.

The literature contains references to a number of excellent computer-assisted advising programs that have been implemented by colleges and universities. One outstanding example is functioning at Brigham Young University (Spencer and others, 1976). Patton (1980) describes the use of the computer at Texas Christian University as a management tool for advisors and advisement administrators. Atkins and Conrad (1977); White, Harvey, and Kethley (1978); Floyd (1974); Pommrehn (1978); McCracken and Penick (1969); Smith (1969); and Vitulli and Singleton (1972) have all described the implementation of various computer-assisted advising programs designed to free advisors from the more perfunctory tasks, giving them time to talk with students about academic and career goals and plans, the essence of the advising process.

Group. More a technique than a delivery system, group advising has been used by institutions as a method of dealing with a large number of advisees in a relatively short time frame. Positive results have been found with group advising. Lewis (1972) reported satisfaction with this approach by students and advisors, more appropriate course selection, and increased retention. Its major advantage is that it is a good way to impart common information in a nonrepetitious fashion (for example, general education requirements, registration procedures, graduation requirements, general career information, decision-making skills, or referral sources), thus freeing the advisor for more substantive contacts with individual advisees. This approach is not used as widely as it probably should be for informational purposes. It obviously lacks the important characteristic of developing the personal and caring relationship between the advisor and advisee that is so critical to good advising.

Self-Advisement. An infrequently used delivery system is self-advisement. In such systems, students are provided with written materials (such as catalogues, handbooks, class schedules, and curriculum guides) and essentially advise themselves in regard to course selection and class scheduling. Institutions favoring this approach do so on the assumption that students are mature and responsible enough to successfully complete this process alone. They cite cost and time efficiencies realized by this form of delivery.

Research on self-advisement has shown that it has been effective when measured against the criteria of fewer enrollment errors (Lewis, 1972; McCoy, 1972; Recer, 1969). Lamb (1980) reported on a successful program of self-advisement at Kapiolani Community College in Hawaii. SAM (Self-Advising Materials), a computer-generated advising program, provides students with the informational materials necessary for making their own course selection decisions. Grites (1979) suggests that a certain amount of self-advisement should be encouraged as a stimulus for more student responsibility in decision making. Thus, self-advisement could strengthen other forms of delivery because students would come to the advising session better prepared to receive advice.

The major weakness of self-advisement, when not supported by other delivery methods, is that it eliminates the opportunity to interact with a helping agent on the important developmental matters of life, academic and career goals, and planning. If one views the major purpose of academic advising as only class scheduling and course scheduling, then self-advisement systems are a workable advising delivery strategy.

Advisement Centers. A more recent delivery system for academic advising is advisement centers. Most have been established within the last fifteen years, although one of the oldest and most successful has been in operation continuously at Ball State University for over thirty years. Baxter (1971) found that enrollment increases and lessened faculty interest in advising were major forces leading to the emergence of advisement centers. Carstensen and Silberhorn (1979) indicated that over two hundred institutions reported they had established advisement centers as a means of delivering advising services to their students. Like other forms of advising, advisement centers are characterized by diversity in their organization and function.

In general, these centralized centers are student service agencies designed to provide accessible information and assist students in their academic decision-making process on a needs basis. They are most frequently staffed by full-time professional advisors, but are often augmented by using faculty on release time or peer advisors and paraprofessionals. A good model for staffing advisement centers with faculty on a part-time basis can be found at the University of North Carolina-Wilmington. Advisement centers have often been designated as the agency to serve the special advising needs of specific groups of students, such as freshmen, undecided or exploratory, handicapped, transfer, returning adult, probationary, and those in the process of changing majors.

Carstensen and Silberhorn (1979) discovered that advisement centers were responsible for a wide range of advising-related functions, including (1) general education advising, (2) advising exploratory students, (3) advising transfer students, (4) running freshman orientations, (5) developing advising handbooks, (6) maintaining advising records, (7) evaluating advising, (8) advising EOP students, (9) advising veterans, (10) providing in-service training for advisors, (11) certifying graduation clearance, and (12) preparing registration instructions and materials.

Some advantages to a centralized advisement center include the following:

- Centralized location accessible to students
- Corp of well-trained advisors
- Continuity of contact
- Specialization of advisors
- Wide range of advising services
- Student rather than departmental centered
- More complete record keeping and monitoring capability
- Accuracy of information for advisees
- Ease of administration, training, supervision, and evaluation

A major disadvantage is often the direct cost of such a center. Shelton (1972) and Pino (1975) have reported positive outcomes of a centralized approach to the delivery of academic advising. Advisement centers have proved to be a workable and effective way to deliver academic advising services to students at a growing number of institutions of higher education.

A Model Delivery System

Academic advising in colleges and universities is characterized by the diversity in personnel and methods used to deliver this important service to students. It is not possible to design a delivery system that will work equally well at all institutions. The key to a successful delivery system is determining which combination of people and methods will work best for a given institution.

I propose a model delivery system for academic advising that incorporates a combination of delivery systems and would be feasible for most institutions. The goal should be adaptation, not necessarily total adoption. Personnel can tailor the concepts presented here to meet their particular needs, resources, and staff capabilities. The model assumes a belief in a student developmental approach to the academic advising process.

A centralized academic advisement center that would serve as a focal point to academic advising on the campus should be established. It would provide a single location, easily accessible to students, where all students could receive ongoing advising relative to their educational and career planning needs at any time convenient to them.

The advisement center staff would develop a campuswide computerized information system designed to provide advisors with timely and relevant information about their advisees.

Staff would consist of a director of academic advising and an appropriate number of full-time professional advisors carefully selected and trained. The staff should have faculty rank and the director would report directly to the chief academic officer of the institution. Adequate clerical staff should also be provided. Full-time staff should be augmented with part-time peer or full-time professional advisors, primarily for information giving, course selection, and scheduling. These individuals would need to be selected, trained, and evaluated on a continuing basis. Peer advisors would also be available to students in the residence halls.

The advisement center would be directly responsible for a variety of advising related functions. Orientation for new students (using group advising techniques), in-service training of peer and faculty advisors, evaluation, development of an information system and advising handbook, and final certification of graduation requirements would all be major responsibilities of the center and its staff.

The advisement center staff would interface closely with other campus referral sources, such as the counseling center, developmental skills, placement, and financial aid. In addition, each of the professional staff would be assigned as a liaison to a college or a group of departments. This would involve communication, training, feedback, and other advising matters.

New students or transfers who had not declared a major would be assigned to an advisor in the advisement center. Freshmen or transfers who were able to declare an intended major at entry would be assigned a faculty advisor in the college or department housing the major. Students who decide to change majors at any time during their college career would automatically be reassigned to the advisement center for further advising. The center would also be the entry point for any special groups of students, such as academically underprepared, returning adults, handicapped, and foreign students.

Faculty advisors within the various colleges and departments would be selected on the basis of their interest and ability as advisors. Not all faculty would advise. The center would provide specialized training to these advisors as needed.

This model incorporates many of the advantages and few of the disadvantages of the various delivery systems reviewed in this chapter.

Summary

Grites (1979, p. 18) captures the essence of the topic when he concludes, "The important determinant is the integration of personnel and techniques. No singular, isolated advising approach can provide all students with assistance in all academic, vocational, personal/social, and administrative matters. Rather than attempting to provide the same advisement for all students, alternative advising schemes should be encouraged."

This chapter has examined various delivery systems and recommended that institutions select a combination of delivery systems most appropriate for their situation and student body.

In the final analysis, although the way institutions choose to deliver advising services to students is important, more important are the institution's commitment to the process and the ability of individual advisors, whoever they may be, to build quality and meaningful relationships with their advisees.

References

Atkins, C. E., and Conrad, C. F. "Improving Academic Advising Through Computerization." *College and University*, 1977, *53*, 115–123.

Baldwin, R. A. "Student-To-Student Counseling: Final Report." 1975 (ERIC Document Reproduction Service No. ED 116 111).

Barman, C. R., and Benson, P. A. "Peer Advisement: A Working Model at the University of Wisconsin-Superior." In L. C. Higginson and K. D. Cohen (Eds.), *Proceedings of the 4th National Conference on Academic Advising.* Asheville: Western Carolina University, 1980.

Baxter, R. P. "A Study of the Emergence and Functioning of Academic Advising Centers Within Academic Units of Major Universities." *Dissertation Abstracts International,* 1971, *32,* 731A.

Bogard, J. R., Hornbuckle, P. A., and Mahoney, J. "Faculty Perceptions of Academic Advising." *NASPA Journal,* 1977 (Winter), 4-10.

Borland, D. T. "Curricular Planning Through Creative Academic Advising." *NASPA Journal,* 1973, *10,* 211-217.

Bostaph, C. P. "A Study of Student Attitudes Toward Three Different Academic Advising Systems Currently Used in Three Different Undergraduate Schools." *Dissertation Abstracts International,* 1977, *37,* 4157A-4158A. (University Microfilms No. 77-685).

Carstensen, D. J., and Silberhorn, C. *A National Survey of Academic Advising.* Iowa City, Iowa: American College Testing Program, 1979.

Chathaparampil, J. "Student Perceptions of Their Academic Advisement at Michigan State University." *Dissertation Abstracts International,* 1971, *32,* 169A.

Cook, N. J. "The Status of Academic Advisement." Unpublished doctoral dissertation, Indiana University, 1980.

Crookston, B. B. "A Developmental View of Academic Advisement as Teaching." *Journal of College Student Personnel,* 1972, *13* (1), 12-17.

Cummer, J. P. "A Study of Counselee Satisfaction in Relation to the Interest Level of Faculty Advisors in Counseling Activities." *Dissertation Abstracts International,* 1961, *22,* 1083.

Cunningham, C. M. "A Study of Freshmen Students' Satisfaction and Perception of the Academic Advisement Program at Oklahoma State University." *Dissertation Abstracts International,* 1975, *35,* 6424A.

Dameron, J. D., and Wolf, J. C. "Academic Advisement in Higher Education: A New Model." *Journal of College Student Personnel,* 1974, *15,* 470-473.

Delworth, U., Sherwood, G., and Casaburri, N. *Student Paraprofessionals: A Working Model for Higher Education.* Washington, D.C.: American College Personnel Association, 1974.

Dressel, F. B. "The Faculty Advisor." *Improving College and University Teaching,* 1974, *22,* 55-58.

Duncan, J. O. "Analysis of the Faculty Advising System of Oregon State University." *Dissertation Abstracts International,* 1973, 1073A-1074A.

Ellison, H. R., Kane, E., and Kelly, W. "Peer-Advising at Three Diverse Educational Institutions." In C. M. Chando (Ed.), *Proceedings of the Third Annual Conference on Academic Advising.* Omaha: Kansas State University, 1979.

Floyd, J. D. "(CAAP) Computer Assisted Academic Advisement and Planning: A Feasibility Study." DeKalb: Northern Illinois University, 1974. (ERIC Document Reproduction Service No. ED 106 674).

Friedman, R. E. "The Advising Structure of McMicken College of Arts and Sciences of the University of Cincinnati and the Institution of Peer Advising Structure: Some Encounters and Observations." In D. S. Crockett (Ed.), *Academic Advising: A Resource Document (1979 Supplement).* Iowa City, Iowa: American College Testing Program, 1979.

Glennen, R. E. "Intrusive College Counseling." *College Student Journal,* 1975, *9,* 2-4.

Grites, T. J. "Student Development Through Academic Advising: A 4 x 4 Model." *NASPA Journal*, 1977, *14* (3), 33–37.

Grites, T. J. *Academic Advising: Getting Us Through the Eighties.* AAHE-ERIC Higher Education Research Report No. 7. Washington, D.C.: American Association of Higher Education, 1979.

Grites, T., and Teague, G. "Faculty Contracts and Academic Advising." *Journal of College Student Personnel*, 1980, *21*, 40–44.

Habley, W. R. "The Advantages and Disadvantages of Using Students as Academic Advisors." *NASPA Journal*, 1979a, *17* (1), 46–51.

Habley, W. R. "Undergraduate Paraprofessionals in Academic Advising: Examining the Program Implications." In D. S. Crockett (Ed.), *Academic Advising: A Resource Document (1979 Supplement).* Iowa City, Iowa: American College Testing Program, 1979b.

Hallberg, E. C. "Realism in Academic Advising." *Journal of College Student Personnel*, 1964, *6*, 114–117.

Hardy, D. C. "Advisement Satisfaction as a Function of Perceived Component Importance, Interpersonal Perceptions, and Self-Perceptions." *Dissertation Abstracts International*, 1976, *37*, 1403A–1404A.

King, M. "Utilizing Part-Time Paraprofessionals as Academic Advisors: A Model." In D. S. Crockett (Ed.), *Academic Advising: A Resource Document (1979 Supplement).* Iowa City, Iowa: American College Testing Program, 1979.

Lagowski, J., and Hartman, N. "Peer Advising: Selection to Evaluation." In C. M. Chando (Ed.), *Proceedings of the Third Annual Conference on Academic Advising.* Omaha: Kansas State University, 1979.

Lamb, M. G. " 'SAM' Academic Advising for the Eighties." *Community Colleges.* University of Hawaii, Office of University Relations, February 1980.

Lewis, W. S. "Self-Advisement Techniques Used in Conjunction with Group and Individual Academic Advisement." *Dissertation Abstracts International*, 1972, *32*, 4956A–4957A.

Looney, S., Anderson, D., and Andrews, P. "Development and Utilization of a Peer Advising Program." In C. M. Chando (Ed.), *Proceedings of Second National Conference on Academic Advising.* Memphis: Memphis State University, 1978.

McCauley, M., and Fletcher, P. "University-Wide Centralized/Specialized Academic Advising—An Integrated Approach." In G. Rayfield, A. D. Roberts, and T. Trombley (Eds.), *Proceedings of the First National Conference on Academic Advising.* Burlington: University of Vermont, 1977.

McCoy, R. D. "Academic Self-Counseling: Does It Work?" *Personnel and Guidance Journal*, 1972, *50*, 834–835.

McCracken, N. M., and Penick, R. J. "Academic Advising at United States Air Force Academy." *College and University*, 1969, *44*, 642–649.

Mash, D. J. "Academic Advising: Too Often Taken for Granted." *College Board Review*, 1978, *107*, 32–36.

Miller, C. L. "Developments in Counseling by Faculty Advisors." *Educational and Psychological Measurement*, 1950, *10*, 451–454.

Murray, J. P. "The Comparative Effectiveness of Student to Student and Faculty Advising." *Journal of College Student Personnel*, 1972, *13*, 562–566.

O'Banion, T. "An Academic Advising Model." *Junior College Journal*, 1972, *42*, 66–69.

Pappas, J. "The Academic Advisement Center: A Model at the University of Utah." In D. S. Crockett (Ed.), *Academic Advising: A Resource Document.* Iowa City, Iowa: American College Testing Program, 1978.

Patton, C. R. "Using the Computer Administratively in Advising." In L. C.

Higginson and K. D. Cohen (Eds.), *Proceedings of the Fourth National Conference on Academic Advising.* Asheville: Western Carolina University, 1980.

Pino, J. A. "The Organization, Structure, Functions, and Student Perceptions of Effectiveness of Undergraduate Academic Advisement Centers." *Dissertation Abstracts International,* 1975, *35,* 4205A–4206A.

Pommrehn, J. D. "Computer-Assisted Degree Progress Reporting." Paper presented at the annual meeting of the American Association of Collegiate Registrars and Admissions Officers, 1978.

Recer, J. D. "Analysis of Alternative Academic Advisement Systems in University College at the University of Oklahoma." *Dissertation Abstracts International,* 1969, *29,* 2495A.

Shelton, J. B. "A Comparison of Faculty Academic Advising and Academic Advising by Professional Counselors: Final Report." Shawnee Mission, Kansas: Johnson County Community College, 1972. ED 065 088.

Smith, H. V. "An Investigation of the Application of Computer-Assisted Instruction and Information Retrieval System to Academic Advising in a Junior College." *Dissertation Abstracts International,* 1969, *30,* 1383A–1384A.

Spencer, R., Peterson, E., Nielson, R. B., and others. "Computer-Assisted Advisement at Brigham Young University." Paper presented at American College Personnel Association Annual Convention, Chicago, 1976.

Titley, B. S. "Academic Advising: Training and/or Educating." In D. S. Crockett (Ed.), *Academic Advising: A Resource Document.* Iowa City, Iowa: American College Testing Program, 1978.

Upcraft, M. L. "Undergraduate Students as Academic Advisors." *Personnel and Guidance Journal,* 1971, *49,* 827–831.

Vitulli, R. A., and Singleton, R. L. "Computer Assisted Advising and Degree Evaluation." *College and University,* 1972, *47,* 494–502.

Walsh, E. M. "Revitalizing Academic Advisement." *Personnel and Guidance Journal,* 1979, *57,* 446–449.

Ward, M., and Higginson, B. "Academic Advising on a Shoestring Budget." In C. M. Chando (Ed.), *Proceedings of the Second National Conference on Academic Advising.* Memphis: Memphis State University, 1978.

White, R., Harvey, I., and Kethley, T. W. "Facilitating Advising Through a Computerized Checklist." *College and University,* 1978, *53,* 164–171.

Zunker, V. G., and Brown, W. F. "Comparative Effectiveness of Student and Professional Counselors." *Personnel and Guidance Journal,* 1966, *44,* 738–743.

David S. Crockett is vice-president, Educational Services Division, the American College Testing Program. He has compiled a comprehensive resource document on academic advising and has conducted numerous national, regional, and individual campus workshops on improving the academic advising process.

The most effective evaluation of an academic advising
program is one that focuses on the advising process.

Using Evaluation to Make Decisions About Academic Advising Programs

Robert D. Brown
Mark J. Sanstead

Good academic advising systems are viewed as a panacea for many of higher education's ills, including depersonalization and high attrition rates (Grites, 1979). The abundant literature on academic advising is replete with descriptions of innovative approaches to academic advising. For the most part, these new models are seldom evaluated. The research literature to date suggests that effective academic advising is related to student persistence in college (Lenning, Beal, and Sauer, 1980; Muskat, 1979), that the frequency of informal contacts with faculty members facilitates the development of a variety of academic skills and improved grade point averages (Morehead and Johnson, 1964; Pascarella and Terenzini, 1978; Terenzini and Pascarella, 1980; Wilson and others, 1975), and that academic advising has a positive influence on the career decisions and educational aspirations of students (Feldman and Newcomb, 1969). Good advising programs also have the potential to influence how satisfied students are with their college experience (Astin, 1977; Pantages and Creedon, 1978; Pascarella and Terenzini, 1977). Finally, the research literature suggests that academic advising facilitates student development (Abel, 1978;

R. Winston, S. Ender, T. Miller (Eds.). *New Directions for Student Services: Developmental Approaches to Academic Advising,* no. 17. San Francisco: Jossey-Bass, March 1982.

Friedenberg, 1950; Hardee, 1962, 1970; Kramer and Gardner, 1977; Robertson, 1958; Yelaja, 1972).

There is no doubt that more research is needed to determine what comprises effective academic advising. However, those who have to make decisions about how to change and improve their academic advising program cannot wait for more definitive answers. They must act on the best information they can accumulate about their college's advising system.

Evaluation for Decision Making

Three fourths of all institutions do not have a formal evaluation process for their academic advising programs. Of those that do conduct formal evaluations, fewer than three fourths conduct them on an annual basis (Carstensen and Silberhorn, 1979). It is difficult to determine how much of this is attributable to a lack of faith in evaluation or a lack of commitment to advising.

There are two major weaknesses of most evaluation efforts, including the studies cited earlier: First, the measures of success (retention and academic achievement) are too global. Both retention and academic achievement are the result of a complex variety of factors of which advising is only one. Second, the evaluation focus is almost exclusively on outcome measures rather than on process variables. Evaluating an academic advising system by assessing its impact on outcome measures is like evaluating a marriage using longevity and the number of children as criteria. Much more goes into the process of a happy marriage and much more goes into making an effective advising system.

The Role of Evaluation. The primary evaluation role is providing information that is useful for decision making about academic advising programs. The information should help decision makers improve the advising system and determine whether some dimension or component of the program should be retained, expanded, or terminated. Emphasizing decision making does not guarantee that every evaluation finding will dramatically shape decisions, but it enhances the possibility that the information will at least reduce the decision maker's uncertainty (Braskamp and Brown, 1980; Patton, 1978). Decisions about academic advising programs are undoubtedly influenced by budget considerations and college politics, as well as by institutional mission and philosophy.

The Decision Makers. It is essential to know who the decision makers are if the evaluation of an advising program is to be useful. Is the decision maker an administrator? Will the faculty be involved? Will there be a vote on the decision? Will an external board be asked to provide guidance for the decision? Is the decision maker the person in charge and the person held accountable? If these are two different people, it is important to know who they are.

Different decision makers have different information needs. The administrator may want to know how the advising program is organized, how much will it cost, who is responsible, and how much management time and how many persons are involved. The faculty may want information about how often students and advisors meet, how effective group advising and written materials are, and what the reward system is for being an effective advisor. An external board may want information on how much the program costs compared to other options.

Evaluators cannot always rely on the person who asks them to conduct the evaluation to be the ultimate decision maker. A dean might request an evaluation of the advising program, but the ultimate decision makers may be department chairpersons, who in turn may be highly influenced by faculty opinion. To consult only the dean about what information is important would result in an incomplete evaluation with little chance for the findings being helpful or even used.

Level of Commitment. Many institutions do little more than provide a lip service commitment to their academic advising program. Half of all faculty contracts do not mention academic advising as a required faculty duty (Teague and Grites, 1980). Many colleges do not take the task seriously enough to provide special attention or a reward system (Ginzberg, 1971). On the other hand, successful advising programs usually have clearly publicized and overt administration support (Daniels and Kiernan, 1965).

The relationship between evaluating the effectiveness of an academic advising program and the level of commitment is a critical one. The greater the commitment, the more likely the institution is going to be receptive to changes designed to improve the advising system. An institution with a high commitment level is also more likely to help an evaluator collect information and utilize evaluative information for decision making.

The level of commitment can be indicated by the willingness to adopt a statement of goals for the program, to establish a committee to oversee an advising program, to conduct a needs assessment to determine faculty and student perceived needs, to provide the necessary resources to implement the program, and to designate someone as accountable. Deciding to conduct an evaluation may itself be substantial evidence of commitment. Commitment can also be indicated by provision for a faculty reward system that encourages and rewards good advising. An institution that sponsors in-service training workshops for faculty and makes available timely and useful information on academic regulations or career development materials is clearly indicating a high level of commitment. Behavioral indexes of commitment, which most of these illustrations are, are better than platitudes on paper.

Faculty commitment must also be assessed. Like the assessment of institutional commitment, behavioral measures are better than attitudinal measures. Do faculty members post advising hours? Do departments hold advising orientations for new faculty members? How much time do faculty members spend on advising? Do faculty members seek out students who do not make appointments? Do faculty members know academic regulations and campus resources for help? Answers to these questions provide an index of level of commitment.

Goals. Most advising programs do not have written objectives (Duncan, 1973). Once the evaluator has determined who the decision makers are, the next step is obtaining their expectations for the program. As noted earlier, the goals are likely to be too global and almost entirely outcome oriented. If this is the case, the evaluator may need to assist the decision makers in clarifying and refining the goals. Ask the decision maker if it would be possible to form an advisory group to examine the goals if they are already in writing or to prepare a goal statement that integrates the goals with the institutional mission and actual advising activities. Input should be sought from alumni, students, faculty, administrators, and key staff, such as those involved in freshman orientation and registration.

Student and Faculty Expectations. Needs assessment data can be useful information to assist an institution to establish goals and priorities for an advising system. Needs assessment data can be obtained directly from available archival records as well as from students and faculty. The number of undecided students, students who change majors, course withdrawals, and underachievers are examples of information that is available without surveying students or faculty. Information from students about their confusions, information needs, sources of help, perceived accessibility of their advisors, and comfort level with their advisor can be additional useful information obtained through interviews and surveys.

Faculty perceptions of students needs should not be ignored. What kind of questions do students ask? What skills do faculty members think they lack in assisting students? Do they believe they have enough time or enough information? What do they consider the goal of advising? These perceptions might be obtained through a survey, but interviews with recognized successful advisors can also provide rich data for use in considering the needs of an advising program.

Decisions. There are two types of decisions to be made about advising programs: decisions about what can be done to improve the advising system and decisions involving choosing among advising programs or program components. The first decision calls for information about ways to improve the program. There are formative evaluations designed to focus on the advising process. Often there are decisions that must be made early. Information is needed at regular intervals to determine how well the program is functioning.

Decisions about choosing between programs, that is, summative evaluations, are designed to assist decision makers in arriving at final judgments affecting the life of an advising program. These evaluations are more likely to include outcome data. Summative evaluations of advising programs include information about student satisfaction and retention rates (Kapraum and Coldren, 1980). Both formative and summative evaluations might examine entire programs or program components, and both could focus on personnel as well as programs. The strategies presented in the following pages apply to either an entire advising system or components. For the most part, however, the emphasis is on evaluating the program rather than people. Table 1 summarizes some major distinctions between formative and summative evaluations.

Evaluation for Improvement

Information about the advising process is most helpful for a formative evaluation. A formative evaluation requires a full understanding of the context in which the advising program takes place. This necessitates answers to the key evaluation questions noted earlier. It also requires a full description of what is expected to happen and what actually does happen during the advising process. If it is possible to make changes while the advising program is being planned and throughout its implementation, the evaluator must be involved in the planning process. It may be difficult to monitor an advising program on a day-to-day basis, but quarterly and semester feedback is essential. The evaluator must monitor the program to see that planned events occur, diagnose problems when something goes wrong, and be able to suggest remedial or trouble-shooting action when necessary.

Formative evaluations can be conducted by on-campus persons, perhaps even a staff member. The primary objective for a formative evaluation is to provide timely information that will help the program succeed. This is accomplished best by someone knowledgeable about the program and readily available.

It is particularly important in a formative evaluation to know the subtasks necessary to achieve an advising objective, as well as the overall objective. This may necessitate a task analysis, resulting in a flowchart outlining the steps necessary to reach an objective. For example, if one of the goals is to assist students in making viable career choices, there are a number of subtasks. The student must know his or her skills, abilities, and interests. This may necessitate a visit to the testing service. The student must also know something about careers related to the tested interests and abilities. This may require browsing in a career library. Finally, the self-knowledge and the career awareness have to be integrated and related

Table 1. Comparisons Between Formative and Summative Evaluations[a]

Areas	Formative	Summative
1. What decisions have to be made?	How to improve advising program	Choosing between two advising programs
2. Who does the evaluation?	Internal staff person	Someone external to program
3. When is evaluator involved?	Early in program planning	Early, but not absolutely necessary
4. What is the role of the evaluator?	Facilitate program success	Provide information for decision making
5. What is the primary focus of the evaluation?	Monitoring program process	Advising outcomes
6. To whom is the evaluator accountable?	Program developers	Program decision makers
7. What methodology is used?	Observations, interviews, anecdotal information	Test results, student records, questionnaires
8. What evaluation design is used?	Naturalistic inquiry	Experimental
9. What does the evaluator need to know about program?	Advising process and procedures	Outcome goals for advising
10. What type of report will the evaluator make?	Informal, periodic oral reports	Formal, written reports
11. What is the primary advantage?	Utility and practicality	Objectivity
12. What is the primary disadvantage?	Weakens credibility for external reviewer	Less utility for helping a program improve

[a] These distinctions are more in terms of emphasis than sharply defined differences.

educational plans must be made. This demands a unique expertise for an advisor.

The same task analysis can be performed for other objectives. If the goal is to assist students in registering, the registration process needs to be clear and timely and the registration materials need to be readily available. If the goal is for students to feel someone within the institution is personally interested in their welfare, this requires advisors who are interested in advising, readily accessible to students, capable of establishing rapport, and good interpreters of school regulations and expectations. There must also be ample opportunity for meetings between advisors and students.

Advising systems differ from campus to campus in intent and implementation. It is thus impossible to describe a detailed task analysis of the advising process that will apply to all campuses. However, it is possible to describe several processes and components and delineate appropriate information needs.

Advisors

Selection. On many campuses, faculty members are expected to be advisors for students majoring in related fields of study. Some campuses, however, have special advising staff for all students or assign freshmen to certain faculty members. The rationale for the selection of advisors should be explicit, and if a new advising program is implemented or the advising program is undergoing special scrutiny, this is an appropriate time for a review of the selection process, criteria, and rationale.

Skills. Undoubtedly, most advisors know their teaching field, but do they know the requirements for majoring in their field? Do they have current information about career opportunities? Do they know general graduation requirements, academic prerequisites, registration deadlines, and the steps students must follow to register? Are faculty members aware of campus resources that assist students who are having academic problems, who face career indecision, or who find financial or emotional difficulties interfering with their performance? What about listening skills and the ability to establish rapport with students? Advisor skills are a critical dimension for any advising program.

Attitudes. The importance of faculty commitment was discussed earlier. Do faculty have the time, interest, and motivation to be effective advisors? These must be determined behaviorally as well as through questionnaires. Faculty may vote in favor of a new or expanded advising program, but may not support it by doing such things as putting schedules on their doors or abiding by them.

Process

Assignment. How are advisor-student assignments made? What kind of first contacts are there with advisors? Do students make individual appointments or do they start off with a group session? Do students have the same advisor for four years? What is the process for changing advisors?

Scheduling. How frequently do students see advisors? How are the sessions initiated? Do they occur at certain times during the semester? How easy is it for a student to see an advisor? How long are the sessions? How long does a student have to wait to see an advisor? How do students go about seeing advisors, do they call, make appointments, drop in?

Content. Content is the core of the advising process. What is discussed during the sessions? Who decides what to discuss? Do advisors refer students to other sources, offer specific advice, assign students tasks? The therapeutic process has been studied extensively, but little is known empirically about what goes on in an advising session. An entire evaluation effort could be focused on this process alone.

Resources

Advising. What kind of resources are available to assist the advising process? Potential resources range from college catalogue to career information. They might also include referral agencies, such as counseling centers, learning centers, and tutorial services. It may not be a function of advising program evaluation to evaluate these resources, but their availability and the advisor's awareness of their existence and how to refer students to them appropriately should be evaluated.

Training. What in-service programs are offered? What written materials are available? Are workshops required or optional? These kinds of questions must be examined to describe and evaluate the effectiveness of advisor orientation programs and written materials on advising procedures.

In summary, these are examples of advising program components that must be considered when planning and conducting an evaluation. It is apparent that what at first may seem like a relatively simple and straightforward activity, that is, academic advising, is a complex enterprise. The evaluator needs to consider the relative importance and effectiveness of the components and interrelated activities, as well as the total program.

Data Collection and Reporting. Because each institution's advising programs are unique and the evaluation questions of interest vary, it is not possible to describe in detail the type of questionnaires and interview schedules that would be appropriate for all settings. A valuable source of advising literature, examples of questionnaires, and an annotated bibliography are available through the American College Testing Program (Crockett, 1978). These materials and samples obtained from other colleges may help evaluators and planners think about the important issues, but persons on each campus will want to design their own evaluation instruments. It is essential that the instruments be designed to answer the evaluation questions of concern to the decision makers rather than depending upon the instruments to shape the questions.

An effective approach to data collection as well as data presentation is the case study approach. This method can be used for either formative or summative evaluations. Describing the plight, for example, of one student trying to make decisions about courses by sorting through the college catalogue, examining registration materials, trying to find the advisor, making an appointment, sorting through the decision with the advisor, and then registering and attending the course can provide a report that has more meaning than tables summarizing attitudes and number of advising sessions. Logs, diaries, interviews, role playing, or following a student around during the registration process provides information for use in case studies.

Here are two examples of case studies based on observational and interview data.

John recently received registration materials for the second semester of his freshman year. He is uncertain about which math course he should take. He is not sure if his high school background is sufficient to handle calculus and is unclear about how much math he needs to graduate. He is also giving some thought to switching to a field of study that would require calculus. He stops by his advisor's office, but no one is there. There is no schedule on the door and the department secretary coldly reports that Dr. Jones is gone for the day. The next day he waits outside the classroom in which his advisor is teaching and tries to catch him after class. While on the go, the advisor tells him he needs one year of math and it does not make any difference what the specific courses are. He signs John's blank registration form and tells him he is free to take whatever course he wants.

John remains uncertain and rather lost as to how to make up his mind. He discusses the problem with his roommate, a college junior, who suggests that John take as little math as possible and wait until the last minute to take more, if it is necessary. John takes no math. At the end of the year he discovers that physics is required for his new career goal, but he must have a full year of math first. He is discouraged and decides to drop out of school for a year.

Contrast John's experience with Mary's.

Mary is a freshman in the nursing program. She is doing well academically and is considering switching to premed. She wonders if she could try it out before making a full commitment, but she is concerned about losing time if she moves completely away from nursing and later decides to return to it.

Mary checks with her advisor, who is out of the office. There is an advisee sign-up sheet; so she makes an appointment for two days later. In the meantime, she stops by the central advising office for nursing students and picks up several brochures that describe alternative science careers and their requirements. She notices one of the major differences between her planned program for next year and the premed program is the addition of premed chemistry and physics.

When she visits her advisor, they discuss the options open to her. She discovers, after the advisor makes a phone call, that she could get credit for premed chemistry if she took a special examination after regular chemistry or sat in on premed chemistry rather than the regular chemistry. She would have to make up the physics, but a summer course that would enable her to work at the same time is available. Her advisor suggests this would be a good way to assess her motivation and ability. The advisor also suggests she talk with someone at the career planning office. She schedules another appointment in two weeks to discuss other ways she can find out more about her interests. Mary eventually switches to premed. She has since recommended the nursing program to several high school students.

These descriptions illustrate what happened in two different advising systems more dramatically than would tables filled with percentages and statistics. Case studies can stand alone as descriptions of advising systems or they can be used to supplement data obtained and presented in other forms. Special care needs to be taken to ensure that the case studies are representative. There are several excellent resources for using qualitative methods for evaluation (see Patton, 1980).

Regardless of the type of information collected or the purpose of the evaluation, it is important that the report be readable and of value to the decision makers. Seldom does the traditional research journal format provide the most effective way for reporting evaluation information. Reports should focus on the decisions and be presented in an understandable manner (see Brown, 1978).

Summary

The most useful evaluation approach assists decision makers in making decisions about the advising process. Global outcome measures, such as retention rates and academic success, can be useful in summative evaluations involving comparisons between two advising systems. However, even in these situations, global outcome measures should not be used exclusively. Those charged with evaluating advising systems should focus on dimensions of the academic advising system that range from the institution's commitment to what actually goes on in the advising session. Good advising systems, like good marriages, may be made in heaven. Understanding the process that makes them work, however, may be the best approach to helping make them better.

References

Abel, J. "Academic Advising Administration: Contributions to Student-Based Management Practices." *Journal of NAWDAC*, 1978, *41*, 102–105.
Astin, A. W. *Four Critical Years: Effects of College on Beliefs, Attitudes, and Knowledge.* San Francisco: Jossey-Bass, 1977.

Braskamp, L. A., and Brown, R. D. *New Directions for Program Evaluation: Utilization of Evaluative Information*, no. 5. San Francisco: Jossey-Bass, 1980.

Brown, R. D. "How Evaluation Can Make a Difference." In G. Hanson (Ed.), *New Directions for Student Services: Evaluating Program Effectiveness*, no. 1. San Francisco: Jossey-Bass, 1978.

Carstensen, D. J., and Silberhorn, C. *A National Survey of Academic Advising.* Iowa City, Iowa: American College Testing Program, 1979.

Crockett, D. S. (Ed.). *Academic Advising: A Resource Document.* Iowa City, Iowa: American College Testing Program, 1978.

Daniels, P. R., and Kiernan, I. R. "Faculty Counseling at F.I.T." *Junior College Journal*, 1965, *36*, 32-35.

Duncan, J. O. "Analysis of the Faculty Advising System at Oregon State University." *Dissertation Abstracts International*, 1973, *34*, 1073A-1074A.

Feldman, K., and Newcomb, T. *The Impact of College on Students.* San Francisco: Jossey-Bass, 1969.

Friedenberg, E. Z. "The Measurement of Student Conceptions of Role of a College Advisory System." *Educational and Psychological Measurement*, 1950, *10*, 545-568.

Ginzberg, E. *Career Guidance: Who Needs It, Who Provides It and Who Can Improve It.* New York: McGraw-Hill, 1971.

Grites, T. J. *Academic Advising: Getting Us Through the Eighties.* Washington, D.C.: AAHE-ERIC/Higher Education Research Report No. 7, 1979.

Hardee, M. D. "Faculty Advising in Contemporary Higher Education." *Educational Record*, 1962, *42*, 112-116.

Hardee, M. D. *Faculty Advising in Colleges and Universities.* Washington, D.C.: American College Personnel Association, 1970.

Kapraum, E. D., and Coldren, D. W. "An Approach to the Evaluation of Academic Advising." *Journal of College Student Personnel*, 1980, *21* (1), 85-86.

Kramer, H. C., and Gardner, R. E. *Advising by Faculty.* Washington, D.C.: National Educational Association, 1977.

Lenning, O. T., Beal, P. E., and Sauer, K. *Retention and Attrition: Evidence for Action and Research.* Boulder, Co.: National Center for Higher Education Management Systems, 1980.

Morehead, C. C., and Johnson, J. C. "Some Effects of a Faculty Advising Program." *Personnel and Guidance Journal*, 1964, *43* (2), 139-144.

Muskat, H. "Educational Expectations and College Attrition." *NASPA Journal*, 1979, *17* (1), 17-22.

Pantages, T. L., and Creedon, C. E. "Studies of College Attrition: 1950-1975." *Review of Educational Records*, 1978, *48*, 49-101.

Pascarella, E. T., and Terenzini, P. T. "Patterns of Student-Faculty Informal Interaction Beyond the Classroom and Voluntary Freshman Attrition." *Journal of Higher Education*, 1977, *48*, 540-552.

Pascarella, E. T., and Terenzini, P. T. "Student-Faculty Informal Relationships and Freshman Year Educational Outcomes." *Journal of Educational Research*, 1978, *71*, 183-185.

Patton, M. Q. *Utilization Focused Evaluation.* Beverly Hills, Calif.: Sage, 1978.

Patton, M. Q. *Qualitative Evaluation Methods.* Beverly Hills, Calif.: Sage, 1980.

Robertson, J. R. "Academic Advising in Colleges and Universities: Its Present State and Present Problems." *North Central Association Quarterly*, 1958, *32*, 228-234.

Teague, G. V., and Grites, T. J. "Faculty Contracts and Academic Advising." *Journal of College Student Personnel*, 1980, *21* (1), 40-44.

Terenzini, P. T., and Pascarella, E. T. "Student Faculty Relationships and Freshmen Year Educational Outcomes: A Freitter Investigation." *Journal of College Student Personnel*, 1980, *21* (6), 521–528.

Thompson, M. S. *Benefit-Cost Analysis for Program Evaluation*. Beverly Hills, Calif.: Sage, 1980.

Wilson, R., Gaff, J., Dienst, E., Wood, L., and Bavry, J. *College Professors and Their Impact on Students*. New York: Wiley, 1975.

Yelaja, S. A. "Student Advising in Social Work Education." *Journal of Education for Social Work*, 1972, *8*, 64–70.

Robert D. Brown is a professor of educational psychology and social foundations at the University of Nebraska-Lincoln. He has published numerous articles on innovative approaches to evaluation and what affects utilization of evaluative information.

Mark J. Sanstead is a doctoral student in counseling psychology at the University of Nebraska-Lincoln. He is interested in innovative programming in higher education.

All college students can be categorized into some campus subpopulation(s), and their advising needs vary accordingly.

Advising for Special Populations

Thomas J. Grites

Just as the academic advising delivery systems, the necessary advisor skills and competencies, and the impacts of academic advising programs vary, so do the students being advised. No one delivery system or single set of skills can be expected to meet the advising needs of all students in our institutions.

These students differ in their ages, sexes, ethnic and religious backgrounds, socioeconomic levels, prior educational experiences, abilities, maturity, interests, expectations, motivations, values, and intended fields of study. During the college experience, they undergo changes in many of these characteristics, and the academic advisor is challenged with continual opportunities to facilitate these changes. By meeting this challenge, the advisor contributes not only to students' immediate growth, but, more important, to their overall ethical development and integrity, their critical thinking skills, their interdependence and humanitarian concerns, their interpersonal competencies, their capacity for intimacy, and their basic sense of identity as described by Chickering (1980).

Unfortunately, many advisors are unaware of the opportunities they have, primarily because they have perceived advising as an administrative, rather than an instructional, responsibility. Historically, advisors merely had to verify student course selections that would fulfill the graduation

R. Winston, S. Ender, T. Miller (Eds.). *New Directions for Student Services: Developmental Approaches to Academic Advising*, no. 17. San Francisco: Jossey-Bass, March 1982.

requirements already published in the college catalogue. To shift to an instructional, developmental concept of advising is no easy transition.

One way to begin this transition is to focus on the identification and understanding of the various populations and subpopulations of students who attend our institutions. Once the advisor has identified and somewhat understood these students, he or she can employ different advising techniques and strategies to design educational environments that will facilitate growth. Academic advising will then become a developmental process for all students. This process will become a developmental one for advisors as well, as they learn more about students' various, yet integrated, growth capacities, as they realize their potential for promoting this growth, and as they actualize their efforts to produce it.

Various terminologies, typologies, and even stereotypes have been used to identify different categories of college students, often with dichotomies implied. Transfer versus native, traditional versus nontraditional, undecided versus decided, women versus men, and handicapped versus nonhandicapped students illustrate some of these dichotomies. Considering still others like preprofessional, international, veteran, nonmatriculated students, and student athletes, it is accurate to suggest that *every* college student can be categorized into some special subpopulation on the campus. The advising needs of each of these categories of students must be assessed and met.

On many campuses, these needs have been accommodated through "special" advising services, offices, and/or advisors. For example, intensive monitoring programs have been initiated for students in the high-risk category (Clayton and Goodrich, 1977); advising centers for undecided students have increased significantly in the last ten years (Pino, 1975); and special advisors have been identified for preprofessional students (especially in the health professions), foreign students, and student athletes. This specialized approach is one method of ensuring that each category of students is uniquely and adequately provided the advising it needs.

However, most students are actually identified by a number of the categories mentioned. To expect specialized advising services for all possible categories would be unreasonable, and to route students to separate offices or advisors for each advising need would be inefficient. An alternative delivery system for advising this wide range of "special" student populations is through individual, adaptive, "developmental" advisors. The advisor who is able to identify the advising needs and characteristics of the various student populations mentioned can in turn alter the advising strategies, techniques, and skills in order to maximize each students' total development. Four categories of students will be examined in some detail. These categories include returning adult students, high-risk students, honors students, and student athletes. Implications and directions for the future development of advising programs are also provided.

Returning Adult Students

Many students have been classified as "nontraditional," but those most often identified as such are the twenty-five-year-old and older students, especially women. Magarrell (1981) reported that this older group of students currently represents more than one third of our campus enrollments. An even larger portion is predicted as a growing concern for lifelong learning evolves, as technological obsolescence increases, and as recruitment efforts are targeted for this group (Kasworm, 1980). Most of these students are returning to college after interruptions due to raising families, military service, or full-time employment; some are experiencing college for the first time; and many are attempting these challenges concurrently. The role of the academic advisor for these students can be critical, especially in a traditional campus setting.

Characteristics. Beyond the delayed reentry or deferred initial entry status of these students, many other characteristics appear to be relatively common among them. Many older students attend on a part-time basis, usually in the evening; many attend with strong external pressures placed on them by their families or employers. They tend to spend comparatively little time on campus other than to attend classes, and they rarely attend or participate in extracurricular activities; they feel out of place, lack self-confidence, have poor study skills, and avoid seeking assistance from available campus agencies. On the positive side, older students often have very specific educational goals, are highly motivated to achieve (although sometimes unrealistically), and bring a broad range of prior life experiences as a framework from which to relate their new learning activities (Kuh and Sturgis, 1980; Rawlins, 1979).

Returning women students, in particular, exhibit characteristics that require specialized advising considerations. Most older women students suffer from both curricular and geographic limitations having been placed upon them. For generations, the stereotypic myth that women's academic skills and abilities were innately void of mathematical and scientific competencies has precluded their opportunity to succeed in certain areas of the college curriculum. Those who have returned in order to improve their employment capability are still usually limited by their geographic immobility due to family commitments. Many have decided to reenter for self-improvement reasons, and the opportunities to develop expansive learning experiences for them are limitless.

Nontraditional students' advising needs and concerns are further inflated because most of the characteristics mentioned coexist with many of the same concerns of younger, traditional students. Ancheta (1980) found that both traditional and nontraditional students sought academic/educational counseling, career/vocational counseling, and personal/social counseling in approximately the same percentages.

These additional concerns suggest that more advising time is required for these students. However, Hines, Krause, and Endieveri (1980) found that the median advisor/student ratio with full-time students in the New York State community colleges was one to twenty; it was one to fifty with part-time students. The implication of this finding is that part-time students require less advising time. Because many nontraditional students attend part-time, yet may have greater advising needs, it is not surprising that they do not perceive their college environments as being very supportive or tolerant of individual differences (Kuh and Sturgis, 1980). Reehling (1980) found that only 1 of 166 returning women students cited encouragement from faculty members or advisors as a reason for continuing their education.

Academic advising for these students becomes very important and complex as both the students and their advisors face transitions requiring new adaptations, reassessments, identities, and intimacies. For example, returning adults will need both intellectual assistance and psychological support in assessing their prior and future learning experiences, in understanding the learning conditions they have not experienced for some time, in knowing the available campus sources of assistance, and in managing their family, work, and educational commitments.

Strategies. Because the nontraditional student presents certain unique characteristics, the advisor needs to be more aware of and better informed about the complexities of their lives. The first step in developing a strategy for advising these students, then, is to learn more about them. This can be accomplished through group advisor training programs, but is best achieved individually as the advisor meets with the student. In order to obtain much of this information, the advisor may need to use an intrusive advising approach. This approach is characterized by an active, dynamic, inquisitive advisor who asks many questions to assess the student's educational and personal backgrounds and who seeks to meet students in places other than the office. This is contrary to "traditional" advising sessions during which the advisor merely responds to student questions during office hours.

Once the advisor has gained knowledge from the student about his or her motivation for attending, previous educational experiences, current educational fears or anxieties, future educational or career plans, and potential conflicts with or support from family or employer, an advising plan can be formulated. This plan is not a simple set of courses already mapped by the catalogue, but rather a coordination of learning experiences that emanate from various sources. The advisor examines the student's background and personal situation and assists in integrating classroom, advising, interpersonal, social, and family interactions into a cohesive educational experience.

The most frequent of these sources will be the classroom, where a broad spectrum of instructional methodologies, expectations, and styles will be introduced. Some will differ significantly from what older students have previously experienced. These variations include contract learning, independent study, computer-assisted instruction, language laboratories, field experiences, and traditional lecture and discussion. In addition, they are usually enrolled in courses along with many younger students who have had recent classroom experience, perhaps with some of these variations in high school; so their uneasiness heightens.

The advising strategy should match the student's characteristics with the most complementary instructional effort. For example, students who need substantial structure in their learning should be directed toward courses that involve participation, regular homework assignments, and frequent assessments. Students who must attend in the evenings, when course offerings are often limited, should consider independent study options that would not conflict with their own commitments, and they should seek out campus activities and programs for the family that might occur simultaneously with their classes. Students who feel inadequate about their study skills and habits should be advised to avoid large lecture courses that require substantial reading, proficient note-taking abilities, and the discipline to study.

Related to the classroom experience is the opportunity to earn college credit by alternative means. Many nontraditional students, particularly those who have substantial work experience, may be eligible for a credit-for-life experience or a credit-by examination (institutional or standardized) option. Others may be able to utilize television or correspondence courses. Except in those institutions designed for nontraditional students and where external degree programs are offered, these alternatives are often unexplored. Fewer than 10 percent of Reehling's (1980) subjects used alternative methods of earning credit other than correspondence study, and only 11 percent used that alternative. Advisors of nontraditional students should be prepared to propose alternative credit options for their students in order to help them accelerate their programs, if appropriate, and to show them the support for these alternatives.

Beyond the classroom, numerous offices, services, and individuals can provide a wealth of educational resources to older students. Financial, psychological or counseling/health, recreational, study skills, and career development services are available to all students; in some institutions, specialized adult student centers and peer or paraprofessional tutoring and advising programs have been established for nontraditional students.

The advisor should, first of all, become familiar with the available resources and then make appropriate use of them through referrals. Students who need tuition deferments or other financial assistance should be referred to the financial aid office to explore potential scholarship, grant, loan, and employment options. Those who have not used their mathematical, writing, reading, or study skills during their absence from an educational environment should be referred to the learning resources center for assistance. Those who have returned to change careers or sample the world of work for the first time should be referred to the career development office for possible workshops, self-help guides, interest and aptitude assessment, and even employment leads. The advisor might send periodic information about such resources to these students in order to make them more aware of and confident in using them.

Because women students, who represent the majority of returning adult students, have suffered from educational stereotyping for so long, the advisor must make a special effort to overcome this. The woman's "place" is no longer in the home; this stereotype is negated as soon as she appears on campus. She is demonstrating her commitment to a new venture. Once she is on campus, the advisor must work to expand her awareness, interests, abilities, and opportunities beyond the historically sex-stereotyped courses, programs, and careers. The advising strategies for these students include the identification of women role models on campus, the encouragement of academic risk taking in curricular areas previously avoided, such as accounting, engineering, mathematics, and the sciences, and the stimulation of confidence in their aspirations and abilities. This will require the same directive, intrusive approach as previously noted and might be facilitated by the assignment of returning women students to female advisors.

The academic advisor must play many roles for the nontraditional student. Beyond program planning, the advisor serves as facilitator, explainer, supporter, assessor, and confidant. Though it is sometimes a difficult task, the rewards of developing these students from a fearful, confused student into a resourceful, confident graduate are enormous.

Programs. A sample of existing programs that focus on the nontraditional student includes the university-without-walls concept at the University of Minnesota and at Empire State College of New York, which uses program advisors, university and community faculty, or clusters of faculty for program planning, documenting prior learning, and developing community-based study projects (Marienau and Eldred, 1978; Shipton and Steltenpohl, 1979). A peer modeling approach for nontraditional students at New Mexico State University has increased their retention through individual counseling and learning assistance (Montes and Ortega, 1976). A telephone tutoring service has met the scheduling, transportation, and childcare needs of nontraditional students at the Community College of Alleghany County (Pennsylvania) Dailey and Jeffress, 1980). The Women's Inner-City Educational Resource Service, Inc. (WINNERS) has provided counseling and other support services and a resource publication for low-income and minority women in Boston (Titterington, 1978). The external degree programs through Thomas Edison College of New Jersey and the Compact for Lifelong Educational Opportunities (CLEO), a consortium of some fifty institutions in the Delaware Valley (Pennsylvania), which provides and coordinates a centralized information access and evaluation center, exemplify two of the more structured and more broadly based assistance programs for adult learners (Niebuhr, 1980; Titterington, 1978).

Academic High-Risk Students

"High-risk students" have been defined in various ways. Educationally or economically disadvantaged, minority, nonnative English speaking, skills deficient, probationary, and even handicapped are terms that have been used to identify high-risk students. One might argue that all first-time college freshmen fall into this category.

Characteristics. The two most common characteristics that high-risk students bring to the institution are fairly obvious. They come to the college environment lacking many of the basic writing, reading, speaking, and computational skills necessary for academic survival, and they are prone to leave the institution prior to graduation (Cope and Hannah, 1975). It is for the latter reason that much attention has been directed to retention programs that concentrate on high-risk students. In addition to skills deficiencies, many of these students may also experience language differences, lack of study space if they live at home, lack of career focus, and actual expectations of failure.

Academic advisors have special challenges and opportunities to create successful developmental experiences for high-risk students. These challenges and opportunities can be met in several ways.

Strategies. Wagner and McKenzie (1980) describe an overall strategy for developing success skills in disadvantaged students that is appropriate for advisors of all types of high-risk students. Although their approach was delivered in a course and classroom format, their overall objectives can be achieved through the advising process as well. Their success strategy initially concentrated on developing the interpersonal skills of nonverbal communication, listening, and responding that would ensure a mutual support system and build confidence in communicating with instructors, librarians, and other campus officials. The next focus was on cognitive skill development, especially through problem-solving techniques. The improvement of reading, writing, speaking, and study skills was given special consideration in this effort.

Although the advisor does not have the luxury of frequent meetings with groups of advisees like an instructor does in the classroom, the same objectives can be achieved. The advisor must be both inquisitive and supportive of high-risk students by assessing and providing the most beneficial learning experiences for them. Specifically, to facilitate students' interpersonal skills development, advisors need to demonstrate their understanding and support of high-risk students by questioning them about their perceived areas of concern, by helping them realize the purposes of an undergraduate education, and by requiring them to engage in communication exchanges with various campus personnel. The use of self-disclosure by the advisor, as well as examples of other faculty and students who might have experienced similar situations as the student being advised, is effective in developing interpersonal skills. The value of peer relationships should also be realized and they should be encouraged.

Cognitive skill development can also be achieved through the advising relationships. The advisor should first help the student determine what factors might inhibit this development by analyzing such possible deterrents as test-taking anxiety, fear of asking for assistance, inability to define problems in concrete terms, or basic skills deficiencies. Once these factors have been determined, the advisor must prescribe specific activities that will enhance cognitive skill development. These can include referrals to special service offices, requesting written feedback from instructors in courses where difficulty is experienced, establishing short-term self-standards for improvements, suggesting participation in other campus activities, and personally reviewing their note-taking abilities. One efficient and effective means to accomplish these activities is through the use of contracts (a negotiated written agreement that specifies the activity, the time allowed for it, and the degree of success expected). Another strategy for advisors is to request midterm progress reports from the student's instructors. Such monitoring need not be institutionalized; individual advisors can initiate such requests on their own.

Minority students offer specific opportunities for the academic advisor. These students need role models, encouragement and support, and exposure to new academic and career areas. The advisor can serve as an intellectual role model or mentor. Walton (1979) posited that having such a model is the single most important element of ethnic minority student retention. He further suggested that ethnic or racial similarities between the student and mentor are unnecessary for a successful relationship as long as genuinely positive attitudes and intellectual abilities prevail. Therefore many advisors can fulfill the mentor role for minority students. One specific effort in this role is to challenge minority students to explore, consider, and sample the academic disciplines and careers they have so long avoided. This should be done, of course, only after the basic college-level reading, writing, studying, speaking, and computational skills have been exhibited.

By using some of the same understandings, skills, and strategies as advisors to nontraditional students, the advisor to high-risk students also serves multiple purposes. Whether acting as planner, helper, evaluator, or advocate, all roles require considerable supportive behavior while still providing the challenges that will facilitate the development of these high-risk students into exemplary graduates.

Programs. Some successful advising programs for high-risk students include the "data-driven advisement model" for minority students, which was introduced at the University of Maryland and is now operable at the University of Illinois at Chicago Circle (Clayton and Goodrich, 1977) and a multidimensional approach to the advising needs of a variety of high-risk students at SUNY-Oswego, which exemplifies the integration of academic and student affairs efforts (Syrell and King, 1979). The Basic Skills and Freshmen Preceptor Programs at Stockton State College (New Jersey) match skills-deficient students with faculty who are both their academic advisor and instructor in a mandated skills course in order to maximize student-faculty contact in both roles (Daly and Grites, 1978). The Retention Advising Program in the College of Liberal Arts at Idaho State University uses carefully selected and trained faculty to advise drop-out-prone students through an intrusive approach (Myers and others, 1979). At Barry College (Florida), advisors to high-risk students have continually reduced attrition through an integrated advising approach of assessing multidimensional student needs and personally contacting individual campus resources to help meet those needs (McDonough, 1980). A variety of peer advising, tutoring, special summer program, and freshman seminars or orientation courses have also been used to reduce the losses of academically high-risk students.

Honors Students

At the opposite end of the student ability continuum is the student whose academic abilities are unquestioned. Students who have entered with exceptionally high test scores, who excel in their classes, and who appear quite able to make their own decisions are often overlooked in the advising process. It is assumed they will meet the established requirements for graduation, find other resources when needed, and proceed through the system without complication. The likely lack of special attention paid these students in the advising process is reflected in the paucity of available literature and research on them. Advisors who do not provide these highly capable students the same time, opportunities, challenges, and assistance as other students are doing them an injustice.

Characteristics. The most obvious characteristic of these students is their exceptional academic ability, at least as measured by previous grades and standardized test scores. As a result of their past academic successes, they are often subjected to exceptional expectations by parents, teachers, themselves, and sometimes advisors. This pervasive expectation creates extreme concerns about maintaining high grades and an overall anxiety to succeed.

Strategies. The academic advisor to honors students has not only exceptional students to advise, but also faces certain exceptional advising situations. The most unique feature of advising honors students is that the advisor must be proficient in advising about failure more often than success. In direct opposition to advising high-risk students, where a positive attitude toward succeeding is critical, advising honors students requires the development of a healthy attitude toward potential failure, heretofore an academic outcome most of them have never experienced.

One of the best overall strategies for accomplishing this advising task is through alternative career planning. Though not easy, this is achieved by indicating that all students, regardless of major, need alternatives in their career plans. Furthermore, all students, regardless of ability or specific career aspiration, have much to learn about life after college and have much to contribute toward society in that life. The advisor should develop a "standard" set of examples to illustrate alternative jobs and careers for various majors.

A corollary to the alternative career strategy is the selection of courses that will enhance those alternatives. These students should be encouraged to use their "electives" to develop special skills that are widely applicable in a variety of work settings. Some combinations might include writing, critical analysis, speaking, foreign language, organizational, and leadership skills. Course selection is also used to ensure the breadth of educational experiences, which is the primary purpose of the undergraduate curriculum.

Lagowski, Hartman, and Bunch (1978) describe several specific advising techniques and tools that are especially appropriate for advising honors students. Because of their exceptional abilities to comprehend information, these students are capable of self-advisement for much of the routine, course-scheduling advising function. This process requires that adequate written information and materials are accurate and available. Self-advisement for specific course requirements allows the advisor more time for discussion with the student about broader educational, career, and/or personal concerns. This does not release the advisor from course selection altogether. The development of broadly applicable academic skills, as mentioned, is accomplished through judicious course selection; the advisor must facilitate that development.

Another advising strategy that is especially effective with honors students is group advising. Advising students in groups of four to ten capitalizes on their comprehension skills, thus also allowing more time for individual advising as necessary. It also provides them an opportunity to understand that they are not alone in their abilities, expectations, anxieties, and career plans. Group advising sessions are especially useful for providing general information about course requirements, available campus resources, application procedures for graduate and professional schools, and other common issues or concerns.

Another strategy that has been adopted in a variety of advising settings and with a variety of student populations is peer advising. Peer advisors for honors students are already aware of and are experiencing much of the same academic competitiveness, frustration, and anxiety; they usually sustain more credibility than faculty and staff because of their more recent firsthand experiences; and they are able to inform faculty and staff about general student needs and concerns. The use of peer advisors should be considered in the overall advising program.

Programs. Most advising programs for honors students seem to be designed for preprofessional students. A few significant ones include the Health Professions Office at the University of Texas at Austin, in which students from high school through those enrolled in foreign professional schools are advised, and the Preveterinary Advising Center at Michigan State University, which has helped to articulate an accountability process for the university, the college, the advising center, the advisors, and the students in determining the impact on students' applications to the admission committee (Lagowski, Hartman, and Bunch, 1978). Thomson (1980) described a computer-assisted advising program for preprofessional students at Marquette University that generates health careers information, graduate programs in biology, admission requirements of medical and dental schools, and an autotutorial advising program for frequently asked information.

Student Athletes

Student athletes have been the subject of much recent controversy. The scandalous disclosures of altered transcripts, grades issued for courses not attended, double admissions standards, and the questionable integrity of some university administrators has heightened the awareness of the unique academic conditions under which student athletes must exist (Austin, 1981; Martin, 1981; Middleton, 1980; Schott, 1981). The National Collegiate Athletic Association (NCAA) has responded to these scandals by imposing stricter academic measures and conditions on athletic programs and the athletes themselves. The advisor to student athletes, as a result, has even greater additional considerations than previously existed for these specially recruited and treated students.

Characteristics. There is a range of student athletes, just like all other categories of students. Those who attract the most attention and publicity are, of course, those in highly competitive athletic institutions whose total college expenses are exchanged for their performance in a sport. Many of these students have high aspirations of playing in the professional ranks and of earning incomprehensible salaries. In addition, there are those who play in institutions with less-glamorous athletic programs, and there are those who simply play for the fun of the game (in intramurals and club sports).

Certain characteristics are common among most types of student athletes, but some are more prevalent in highly competitive institutions. Unusual opportunities for student development are made available through the role of athletics in higher education. Most student athletes must learn to accept criticism, from coaches as well as themselves. They experience exceptional activities in which to demonstrate their cognitive abilities by perfecting skills and their social abilities through leadership. They are able to build high self-esteem to formulate their identities (especially sexual) and to manage their deeper personality needs (especially aggression) (Sanford, Borgstrom, and Lozoff, 1973).

Student athletes are often further characterized by excessive class absences and late assignments due to lengthy practices, team meetings, and road trips. Their inattention to academic work during "the season" is obvious. Those on scholarships are often obsessed by the single career objective of playing professionally. This can result in considerable anxiety about injuries, which could terminate their career plans. Student athletes are also accustomed to special privileges for their meals, registration procedures, academic assistance, and sometimes their grades.

Since 1975, these conditions have not been limited to male athletes. Women's athletic programs have grown substantially since the Title IX section of the Educational Amendments Act was passed. Though still not as heavily funded as men's programs, the recruitment efforts, special considerations, and academic considerations do rival them.

Student athletes, both men and women, may approach the advising situation much differently than most students because of their extremes of commitment, expectations, and previous attention. The advisor to these students has unusual conditions under which to facilitate their development.

Strategies. The NCAA has actually simplified the academic advisor's role by specifying the number of credit hours to be completed each term to retain athletic eligibility. The association further requires that institutions publish their standards for measuring academic progress, that presidents or chancellors be responsible for certifying academic eligibility, that extension and credit-by-examination courses from other institutions be prohibited to athletes, that official academic approval be acquired before athletes enroll in summer courses at other institutions, and that junior college athletes who had less than a 2.0 average in high school must graduate from the junior college before they are eligible for varsity sports in a four-year institution.

Ironically, Martin (1981) has observed that the regional accrediting associations have failed to enforce compliance with certain academic regulations, which have been applied selectively to student athletes. The very agencies with regulatory jurisdiction over these institutions have, by their neglect, risked the integrity and credibility of the overall educational mission. They are tacitly approving of violations of academic policies, the tampering with transcripts, the creation of nonchallenging courses in the curriculum, cheating, and plagiarism. Most sadly, they are ignoring the unpreparedness with which student athletes often enter the world beyond college, whether as a professional athlete or in a less-glamorous career, and the apparent lack of concern about this state. This is of particular concern for minority student athletes, who, contrary to their pipe dreams of fame and wealth, more often find themselves back in their hometowns without a real education and with little fame or wealth.

Where does the academic advisor fit into this scheme? The NCAA and the regional accrediting agencies are not likely to meet with individual student athletes to confront them with the regulations and concerns I have described; the advisor is. By using some of the same strategies used with other students, such as making referrals, prescribing specific activities, and using group and peer advising approaches, the advisor creates learning experiences for the student athlete that carry beyond the playing field.

The academic advisor to student athletes has one advantage because of the direct advising approach that can be used. Student athletes are comfortable with taking specific directions from coaches, and the advisor can employ a similar approach. The specificity in eligibility conditions now required by the NCAA (Middleton, 1980) makes this task even easier.

The difficult task of the advisor to scholarship athletes is to that of advising the preprofessional student, that is, advising about failure and developing alternative career plans. The advisor should attempt to ensure that academic progress is made not only to retain athletic elgibility, but also to advance the completion of a marketable degree that will be compatible with their nonathletic skills. The advising strategy for these students must be one of direct confrontation with the high probability that their professional athletic careers may not develop as planned. Where available, data about the success of the institution's former scholarship athletes, both in professional sports and other areas, should be made known. The need to develop an alternative career plan is obvious, although not always to the students.

The advisor needs to relate the student's athletic experiences to the total college and other life experiences. The advisor should spend time reinforcing students' abilities to learn new skills, to develop leadership qualities, to assume responsibilities, and to work cooperatively with others, skills already demonstrated through their athletic participation.

Recognizing student athletes' likely compulsion for following directions, the advisor has the opportunity to specify certain academic behaviors that will coincide with those in athletics. These behaviors might include referrals for improving their basic academic skills (primarily through tutoring), suggestions to become involved in some other campus activity besides athletics, and requirements that they talk with their instructors *in advance* of foreseeable conflicts between academic work and athletic participation, as well as meeting other student academic responsibilities.

Although student athletes are "conditioned" to follow directions, they may not as readily follow the advisor's directions as the coach's. Therefore, regular monitoring is necessary, especially for the nonplaying athlete who is overly concerned about winning a position. The regular is more concerned with eligibility and therefore is often more receptive to advising about academic success. The same advising strategy may be necessary with coaches, especially if they are not part of the regular college faculty.

There is no question that student athletes comprise a special population of college students. They often bring to the advising relationship some of the same characteristics as the honors students and the high-risk student (unknown failure and a narrow career goal, along with academic skills deficiencies). This unusual combination presents a new challenge to academic advisors. With a lot of understanding and some of the directive advising techniques described, these students can realize the same developmental impact as others. The advisor will need to exercise the initiative to achieve this goal, however, and those who fail to do so will have seriously failed in their responsibilities to ensure a true education for these students.

Programs. The controversy surrounding student athletes is recent; so very little literature on advising programs for them is available. Some of the programs that have attempted to avoid the controversy include those at Old Dominion University (Virginia), where specific goals and objectives of a student athlete advising system have been developed and programs have been implemented to achieve them (Earl, 1979) and at West Virginia University, where a thorough process for advising and monitoring the academic progress of student athletes, including specific responsibilities for all university constituents, is under study. An interdisciplinary program between the counselor education and athletic departments at the University of Virginia, which requires first semester freshman athletes to participate in tutoring, group classes, study halls, and individual counseling sessions, has received favorable responses from counselors, tutors, and the athletes (Cleland, 1981). The prestigious women's athletic program at UCLA lauds its success in producing athletes who also complete their degrees (Lichtenstein, 1981).

Implications

This chapter has reviewed some of the efforts necessary to provide quality academic advising for the special student populations in our institutions. Several general implications can be drawn from this review and should be taken into consideration as institutions examine their advising programs.

First, advisors need to be aware that they may not be effective in advising all types of students. They need to know their particular advising strengths and limitations so that they can be most effective in certain situations and able to make appropriate referrals in others.

Second, the strategy to be employed in any given advising situation must depend on the advising needs of the individual student. Some special groups of students exhibit unique advising needs, but because an individual student may belong to several of these subpopulations, the advisor must assess each one's characteristics and needs independently.

Third, an adequate method of more accurately identifying the advising needs of individual students needs to be developed, rather than merely exploring the common characteristics of categories of students. Polson and Cashin (1981) suggest an "advising needs inventory" or "advising development scale" that would include items relevant to academic decisions and potential academic and personal problems. Gill and Freuhling's (1979) College Student Goals Inventory (CSGI) could provide the basis for such an instrument. The CSGI contains one hundred remedial, developmental, and preventive goal statements in eight goal areas; need is determined by the difference between the student's desire to achieve a goal and perceptions of the institution's assistance in achieving the goal. The academic advisor is an obvious choice to clarify the institutional role and to facilitate the institutional environment to the student's advantage in order to reduce that difference (that is, meet the need).

Finally, the identification of cognitive learning styles should be investigated for its utility in the developmental process of advising. Although this could be yet another way to categorize students, there are potential implications for the matching of students with advisors and for advisors to create the most appropriate learning conditions for their students. These learning styles have been described in various combinations and terms, and several instruments are available to distinguish them (Fuhrmann and Jacobs, 1980; Renzulli and Smith, 1978).

In brief, no matter what advising conditions exist on the campus, the individual academic advisor has a significant opportunity to develop students to their fullest academic and interpersonal potentials. This opportunity is exceptional when advising certain special populations of students.

References

Ancheta, B. "Counseling Needs of Traditional and Nontraditional Community College Students." *Journal of College Student Personnel*, 1980, *21* (6), 564–567.

Austin, A. D. "Bringing Free Enterprise to Big-Time College Sports." *Chronicle of Higher Education,* March 23, 1981, p. 25.

Chickering, A. W. "Adult Development: A Workable Vision for Higher Education." In *Current Issues in Higher Education: Integrating Adult Development Theory with Higher Education Practice,* no. 5. Washington, D.C.: American Association for Higher Education, 1980.

Clayton, R., and Goodrich, A. "Advising Minority Students." In G. Rayfield, A. D. Roberts, and T. Trombley (Eds.), *National Conference on Academic Advising: A Publication of Proceedings.* Burlington: University of Vermont, 1977.

Cleland, G. "Athletes Score Points with Counseling Program" *Guidepost,* March 5, 1981, p. 3.

Cope, R. G., and Hannah, W. *Revolving College Doors: The Causes and Consequences of Dropping Out, Stopping Out, and Transferring.* New York: Wiley, 1975.

Dailey, A. L., and Jeffress, C. A. "Telephone Tutoring for the Nontraditional College Student—A Homework Hotline." *Journal of College Student Personnel,* 1980, *21* (6), 574–575.

Daly, W. T., and Grites, T. J. "Integrating Basic Skills Education and Freshman Advising." In C. M. Chando (Ed.), *Proceedings of the Second National Conference on Academic Advising.* Memphis: Memphis State University, 1978.

Earl, W. R. "Advising the Student Athlete—Special Programs for Special Needs." In C. M. Chando (Ed.), *Proceedings of the Third National Conference on Academic Advising.* Memphis: Memphis State University, 1979.

Fuhrmann, B. S., and Jacobs, R. T. *Learning Interaction Styles: Development, Testing, Uses of an Inventory.* Richmond, Va.: Ronne Jacobs Associates, 1980.

Gill, J. S., and Freuhling, J. A. "Needs Assessment and the Design of Service Delivery Systems." *Journal of College Student Personnel,* 1979, *20* (4), 322–328.

Hines, E. R., Krause, P., and Endieveri, F. J. "Academic Advising in Two-Year Colleges." *Community/Junior College Research Quarterly,* 1980, *4* (2), 151–167.

Kasworm, C. E. "Student Services for the Older Undergraduate Student." *Journal of College Student Personnel,* 1980, *21* (2), 163–169.

Kuh, G. D., and Sturgis, J. T. "Looking at the University Through Different Sets of Lenses: Adult Learners and Traditional Age Students' Perceptions of the University Environments." *Journal of College Student Personnel,* 1980, *21* (6), 483–490.

Lagowski, J. M., Hartman, N. A., and Bunch, J. M. "Advising and Counseling the Preprofessional Student." In C. M. Chando (Ed.), *Proceedings of the Second National Conference on Academic Advising.* Memphis: Memphis State University, 1978.

Lichtenstein, G. "The Wooing of Women Athletes." *The New York Times Magazine,* February 8, 1981, p. 27.

McDonough, E. "Advising High-Risk and International Students." In L. C. Higginson and K. D. Cohen (Eds.), *Academic Advising as a Developmental Process: Proceedings of the Fourth National Conference on Academic Advising.* University Park: Pennsylvania State University, 1980.

Magarrell, J. "The Enrollment Boom Among Older Americans: 1 in 3 College Students Is Now over 25 Years Old." *Chronicle of Higher Education,* May 4, 1981, p. 3.

Marienau, C., and Eldred, M. "Educational Program Planning for Adult Students." In C. M. Chando (Ed.), *Proceedings of the Second National Conference on Academic Advising.* Memphis: Memphis State University, 1978.

Martin, W. B. "Why Won't Accreditors Investigate the Abuses in College Athletics?" *Chronicle of Higher Education,* January 26, 1981, p. 64.

Middleton, L. "NCAA to Vote on Tougher Academic Rules for Athletes. "*Chronicle of Higher Education*, December 15, 1980, p. 1.

Montes, D., and Ortega, L. "Retention of the Non-Traditional Student Through Peer Modeling." Paper presented at the American Personnel and Guidance Association annual convention, Chicago, 1976. (ERIC Document Reproduction Service No. ED 130 214).

Myers, R., Mauch, J., Hill, L., and Williams, M. E. *Retention Advising Program (RAP): A Model for Involving Liberal Arts Faculty as Advisors for Drop-Out Prone Students.* Pocatello: Idaho State University, 1979.

Niebuhr, H., Jr. "CLEO: A New Girl in Town!!!" *Higher Education Planning*, 1980, 7 (4), 1-4.

Pino, J. A. "The Organization, Structure, Functions, and Student Perceptions of Effectiveness of Undergraduate Academic Advisement Centers." Unpublished doctoral dissertation, Temple University, 1975.

Polson, C. J., and Cashin, W. E. "Research Priorities for Academic Advising: Results of Survey of NACADA Membership." *NACADA Journal*, 1981, *1* (1), 34-43.

Rawlins, M. E. "Life Made Easier for the Over-Thirty Undergrads." *The Personnel and Guidance Journal*, 1979, *58* (2), 139-143.

Reehling, J. E. "They Are Returning: But, Are They Staying?" *Journal of College Student Personnel*, 1980, *21* (6), 491-497.

Renzulli, J., and Smith, L. H. *Learning Styles Inventory: A Measure of Student Preference for Instructional Techniques.* Mansfield Center, Conn.: Creative Learning Press, 1978.

Sanford, N., Borgstrom, K., and Lozoff, M. "The Role of Athletics in Student Development." In J. Katz (Ed.), *New Directions for Higher Education: Services for Students*, no. 3. San Francisco: Jossey-Bass, 1973.

Schott, J. L. " 'If You Flunk Billy, It'll Cost Us the Game.' " *Chronicle of Higher Education*, March 23, 1981, p. 25.

Shipton, J., and Steltenpohl, E. H. "A Model for Individualized Degree Program Planning." In C. M. Chando (Ed.), *Proceedings of the Third National Conference on Academic Advising.* Memphis: Memphis State University, 1979.

Syrell, L., and King, D. W. "Specific Responses to High Risk Students at a State College." In C. M. Chando (Ed.), *Proceedings of the Third National Conference on Academic Advising.* Memphis: Memphis State University, 1979.

Thomas, R. G. "Computer-Assisted Advising Programs." *Journal of College Student Personnel*, 1980, *21* (6), 571-572.

Titterington, T. A. "Aiding the Student as Comparison Shopper." In M. Keeton and P. Tate (Eds.), *New Directions for Experiential Learning: Learning by Experience—What, Why, How*, no. 1. San Francisco: Jossey-Bass, 1978.

Wagner, C. A., and McKenzie, R. "Success Skills for Disadvantaged Undergraduates." *Journal of College Student Personnel*, 1980, *21* (6), 514-520.

Walton, J. M. "Retention, Role Modeling, and Academic Readiness: A Perspective on the Ethnic Minority Students in Higher Education." *The Personnel and Guidance Journal*, 1979, *58* (2), 124-127.

Thomas J. Grites is director of academic advising at Stockton State College, Pomona, New Jersey. He has authored various publications on the process of academic advising in higher education. He is currently president of the National Academic Advising Association and chairperson of the American College Personnel Association's Commission I on Organization, Administration, and Development of Student Personnel Services.

The quality of academic advising students'
experiences is directly related to the quality and rigor
of the training of the advisors.

Training Allied Professional Academic Advisors

Steven C. Ender
Roger B. Winston, Jr.

Many institutions question the need to establish training programs for those individuals who serve in the academic advising role. This thinking is short-sighted at best! Research has shown that quality advising is a cornerstone to student retention and satisfaction with the institution (Crockett, 1978a).

Today's colleges and universities are utilizing faculty members, student affairs professionals, student peer advisors, and in limited situations, full-time personnel to offer advising services to students. Both faculty and student affairs professionals can best be classified as allied professionals when serving in the academic advisor role. Allied professionals, as defined by Delworth and Aulepp (1976), are persons with the time and talent to assist others who have an extended educational background in some other profession and bring with them highly developed skills for providing a service, but who may require additional training and supervision in order to deliver a specific service.

This chapter focuses on training allied professionals to serve as academic advisors. Individuals who wish to train peer (paraprofessional)

R. Winston, S. Ender, T. Miller (Eds.). *New Directions for Student Services: Developmental Approaches to Academic Advising*, no. 17. San Francisco: Jossey-Bass, March 1982.

academic advisors are encouraged to consult other sources, such as, Ender, McCaffrey and Miller (1979), Delworth (1978), and Ender and McFadden (1980), for suggestions concerning content and training strategies. It is assumed that full time professional advisors have been educated to perform the advisor functions prior to their employment at the college.

In most instances allied professionals bring the following to the academic advising role: (1) knowledge (in some cases limited) of the academic curriculum, (2) desire and willingness to assist students in meaningful and productive ways, and (3) firsthand experience as a successful student. The purpose of this chapter is to review the roles and functions of the academic advisor, the skills needed to perform in these roles, and the issues which must be addressed if quality training and advising is to occur. The training model presented here is designed to address the training concerns when dealing with allied professional advisors.

The Role and Function of Academic Advising

The primary role and functions the academic advisor might assume have been identified in earlier chapters of this volume. They are briefly reviewed here to focus on their training implications. Before one can consider the types of skills for which training is needed, considerable attention must be focused on deciding what type of advising program the institution will implement and the specific functions the academic advisor is expected to perform. Basically, the academic advising process can be one of two types: prescriptive or developmental (Crookston, 1972). Characteristics of the prescriptive or developmental (Crookston, 1972). Characteristics of the prescriptive model include advice giving, reacting to problems or crises, and relating to students as an authority figure. The developmental model, on the other hand, is based on a different set of values and beliefs. The relationship between advisor and student is central to the developmental model and is one in which both the advisor and student engage in a series of developmental tasks, the successful completion of which results in varying degrees of learning by both parties. Implementation of this approach requires advisor and student to openly and freely reach agreement about such issues as who takes the initiative when, for what does each party assume responsibility, and how does one acquire the knowledge and skills (Crookston, 1972). The relationship is the key to the developmental advising model and is an essential component of the training model.

The critical function the academic advisor must perform in the developmental model is that of a mentor and friend to the student. The functions the advisor who serves as a mentor to students include: (1) facilitating the development of self-responsibility, (2) facilitating a sense of self-directedness, and (3) focusing attention on developmental task achievement with students.

Crookston (1972) advocated four primary roles for academic advisors with specific functions for each role. Similar roles and functions were incorporated in the thinking of Crockett (1978a) and Miller and Prince (1976) and establish the rationale for the training experience. The four major roles and related functions are:

1. *Instructor:* a teacher who helps students to formulate intellectual objectives; establish educational goals; and select courses consistent with the student's intellectual and career interests.

2. *Growth Facilitator:* serves as sounding board for student's personal goals; assists in solving personal problems; helps solve academic problems; provides a personalized educational experience.

3. *Resource Person:* helps students find appropriate helping resources; makes referrals when needed; provide information about various campus and community resources which will help achieve personal goals; and serve as a personal contact for answering questions about their relationship with the institution.

4. *Friend:* serve as a warm, caring individual; becomes a positive force in the student's personal growth and development; and may act as an adult role model for healthy, constructive living.

Essential Advisor Competencies

Crookston (1972) points out five basic competencies which are essential if the advisor is to perform the multiple roles and functions detailed in developmental advising. These competencies and subsequent helping skills or knowledge necessary to serve as an academic advisor provide the framework for training.

Competency One. Advisors are able to initiate, establish, and maintain mutually derived relationships with students which can be characterized as friendly, open, respectful and trusting. The training program should assist advisors in assessing present helping skills' levels, provide an introduction to basic oral communication/facilitation skills (including extensive opportunities for practice) and present a developmental model of academic advising, emphasizing the mentoring relationship.

Competency Two. Advisors are fully conversant with the requirements of various academic programs and the college's academic policies and procedures. The skills needed in this area are primarily cognitive. The advisor must know the requirements of the core curriculum and each major, necessary prerequisite courses, and the subtle differences among the most appropriate sequences of courses for various major areas of study.

Competency Three. Advisors are knowledgable about basic developmental processes, stages and tasks of late adolescence through the middle-age years. This competency is primarily concerned with knowledge of developmental stages and tasks and the ability to help others assess their present levels of functioning. If the advisor is to facilitate the development of self-responsible, self-directed behaviors and focus attention on developmental task achievement, as McCaffrey and Miller (1980) and Crookston (1972) advocate, they must be acquainted with developmental theory and be able to distinguish, through formal and informal assessment techniques, the student's level of development. This is of special importance if the student is facing developmental or remedial concerns which require assistance from helping professionals (for instance, counselors, mental health workers, psychologists).

Competency Four. Advisors are able to teach students how to formulate and write goals and objectives as they impress upon them the value of planning for academic, career, and personal growth. The skills and knowledge requisit for reaching competency in this area include: assessment, goal setting, formulating and writing behavioral objectives, decision making strategies, study skills techniques, career exploration and resource utilization.

Competency Five. Advisors are able to make referrals to other available services and programs. This competency requires a full knowledge of the resources on campus and in the larger community and the ability to make a referral which is viewed by the student as both helpful and necessary and not as rejection, giving them the run-around, or casting them off to someone else.

The Training Program

Training programs should be well planned and have specific outcomes identified. If advisors are to be competent in the variety of roles identified here the following eleven training areas are viewed as essential for an adequate training program.

In order to cover the material in the eleven training areas, a minimum of thirty hours of instruction/training is viewed as necessary. All training areas do not require equal amounts of time devoted to them, however. Each training team will need to make decisions about priorities based on the goals of the program and the skill level of the participants.

Area I. Definition of Academic Advising and Required Roles: Outcome Objectives

1. *Advisors can articulate their mentoring role to students.*

2. *Advisors know the four specific characteristics of their allied professional roles (instructor, growth facilitator, resource person and role model/friend).*

3. *Advisors understand their roles and how they relate to the mission of the college.*

For many individuals participating in the training program, the concept of being a mentor to students may be a new and perhaps threatening role. Some will resist the idea altogether and they should be allowed to drop out of the advising program.

Most of the allied professional participants can identify a mentor in their lives and this process of identification will help them to better understand the power and responsibilities inherent in the advising relationship. The outcome of this training area must focus on the characteristics, roles, and responsibilities of the advisor. If participants fail to grasp the significance of their advising role, subsequent training sessions will be of little importance and the relevance of many of the remaining areas will become suspect. If, on the other hand, participants can conceptualize the kind of advising described here, the importance of subsequent training areas will be apparent.

The first training session is crucial. If a solid base of understanding and agreement about the nature of the advisor roles is not clarified and agreed upon, the rest of the training will be seen as ambiguous at best. Additionally, it is important to point out to advisors that part of their responsibility, when working with advisees, is to communicate clearly the nature of the advisor's role. Students need to understand the services and roles the advisor is qualified and willing to offer for their use. Part of the role is challenging students to take advantage of this unique relationship.

Area II. Knowledge of the College Curriculum, Policies and Procedures: Outcome Objectives

1. *Advisors know and can communicate to students what courses are required to complete core curriculum requirements.*
2. *Advisors can teach students how to use the student handbook, college catalogue and other college policy/information sources.*
3. *Advisors know registration, add-drop and withdrawal procedures.*
4. *Advisors can assist students in developing short- and long-range academic plans.*

For many advisor training programs this area provides the heart of the curriculum. Training in this area, when applied to the developmental model, certainly focuses on ensuring that advisors know the unique characteristics of the academic curricula and the policies and procedures of the institution. The major difference between the prescriptive and the developmental models is that advisors using the latter model, instead of simply telling students the procedures, assist them in discovering the sources of information that may be used now and in the future. The advisor must teach students how to use the institutional handbook, how to develop academic plans, and how to assess their academic strengths and weaknesses so that academic choices reflect the student's abilities and interests. Subsequent training sessions which address assessment and career awareness will have a direct impact on the advisor's ability to serve as a mentor in this area.

Area III. Human Growth and
Development: Outcome Objectives

1. *Advisors understand the developmental stages common to adolescents and adults (that is, identify formation for 18-23 year olds, or reassessment of family and career relationships and responsibilities for 35-43 year olds).*
2. *Advisors know the important developmental tasks of various stages and their implications for academic success.*
3. *Advisors can distinguish between developmental and remedial issues which require the attention of a helping professional.*
4. *Advisors are aware of and can utilize several developmental strategies with individual students.*

The academic advisor is not expected to be an expert in human growth and development but should be aware of the life stages and developmental tasks that their advisees are experiencing. These stages and tasks are different for various age groups, but the literature in human growth and development is substantial so identifying the various stages and tasks is not a cumbersome process. Examination of the works of Heath (1968), Chickering (1969), Levinson (1978), Chickering and Havighurst (1981), and Perry (1970) and others will aid the advisor in understanding the stages and tasks of most students encountered. (See Chapter Two for application of the Perry model.) The important role of the mentor is to help advisees decide if problem areas and concerns are primarily developmental or remedial in nature (see Figure 1.) If the concern is developmental, appropriate strategies can be explored with the advisee (for example, goal setting, decision making, career exploration, resource utilization). Programmatic strategies which might be built into the advising system include using developmental transcripts (Brown and Citrin, 1977; Knefelkamp, 1980) or assessment instruments such as the Student Developmental Task Inventory (Winston, Miller and Prince, 1979b).

On the other hand, if the concern is remedial in nature and one causing extreme anxiety for the advisee, the advisor must recognize these dynamics and make an appropriate referral to a department or agency where appropriate expertise is available. Communication skills, knowledge of developmental stages and tasks, specific helping strategies and knowledge of campus resources and appropriate referral techniques are crucial training areas if the advisor is to assist students with their developmental concerns.

Figure 1. Student Concerns and Sources of Help

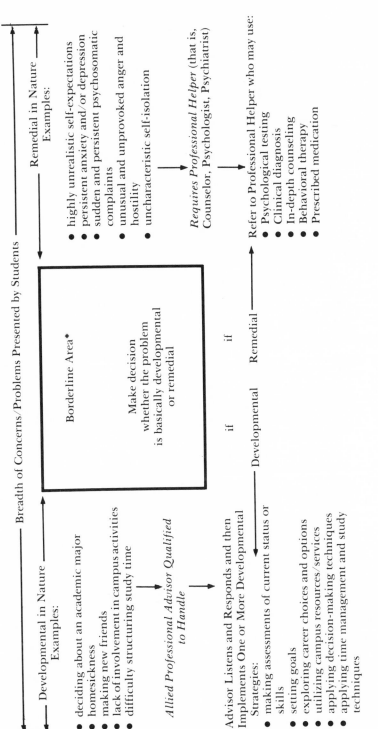

← Breadth of Concerns/Problems Presented by Students →

← Developmental in Nature
Examples: →

← Remedial in Nature
Examples: →

- deciding about an academic major
- homesickness
- making new friends
- lack of involvement in campus activities
- difficulty structuring study time

- highly unrealistic self-expectations
- persistent anxiety and/or depression
- sudden and persistent psychosomatic complaints
- unusual and unprovoked anger and hostility
- uncharacteristic self-isolation

Allied Professional Advisor Qualified to Handle

Requires Professional Helper (that is, Counselor, Psychologist, Psychiatrist)

Borderline Area*

Make decision whether the problem is basically developmental or remedial

if   if

Developmental   Remedial

Advisor Listens and Responds and then Implements One or More Developmental Strategies:

- making assessments of current status or skills
- setting goals
- exploring career choices and options
- utilizing campus resources/services
- applying decision-making techniques
- applying time management and study techniques

Refer to Professional Helper who may use:

- Psychological testing
- Clinical diagnosis
- In-depth counseling
- Behavioral therapy
- Prescribed medication

*Borderline concerns are generally of a "counseling" nature and do not require intensive psychotherapy. These concerns usually revolve around interpersonal conflicts. Advisors when confronted with these types of issues have responsibility to be empathetic listeners and sounding boards. In many instances, students will resolve interpersonal conflicts by "talking out" these issues with a supportive person.

Area IV. Communications Skills: Outcome Objectives

   1. *Advisors can demonstrate active listening techniques.*
   2. *Advisors can serve as a sounding board for students.*
   3. *Advisors can demonstrate the ability to give empathic, interchangeable responses.*
   4. *Advisors can determine if students' problems are developmental or remedial in nature.*

The ability to use appropriate communications skills while interacting with advisees is crucial to developing a trusting, meaningful working relationship. The key to the relationship is the genuineness of the advisor. If genuineness is evident, the advisor will recognize the feelings students have about the various facets of their relationships with the institution, their studies and important people in their lives such as parents, peers and teachers. Many communications experts call this "being a sounding board" for a person (Gazda, and others 1973; Carkhuff, Pierce and Cannon, 1977) and is an essential element in helping an individual work out personal problems. If the problem is of a developmental nature the advisor may introduce strategies such as goal setting, establishing behavioral objectives, decision-making techniques, etc. If the problem is of an anxiety-producing nature, listening and giving empathic responses is the initial role of the advisor. If the student does not reach satisfactory conclusions or solutions, referral to appropriate helping agencies is the appropriate next step to take. Figure 1 illustrates the possible choices open to the advisor when working with developmental or remedial concerns.

As advisors listen to students' concerns and problems, they serve as sounding boards for students' self-explorations. During this initial phase of helping, the advisor begins making determinations as to whether the problem is primarily developmental or remedial in nature. If the problems seem to be of a developmental nature, the advisor may attempt to initiate specific developmental strategies with the student (for instance, goal setting, study skills, career exploration). On the other hand, if the problems seem to be more remedial in nature, the advisor's responsibility is to listen, assist the student in self-exploration and oftentimes make referrals to a resource that is designed to aid students in overcoming obstacles which interfere with their ability to cope in the college environment.

Even though many developmental concerns will require the utilization of campus resources beyond the advisor, remedial type concerns mandate a referral to more specialized helpers. The advisor may want to consider three specific questions when making the decision about whether to initiate helping strategies, or to refer.

   1. Is the student's behavior basically functional or dysfunctional? Is the student able to meet general responsibilities (for instance, eating, sleeping, attending classes, maintaining personal hygiene), or is the prob-

lem severe enough to interfere with these basic activities? If the latter is the case, the advisor should take steps to help the student receive attention from a professional helper.

2. Is the problem centered in the present or does it have historical antecedents? Is the problem a relatively recent one that is directly related to the present environment, or is it a long-standing problem (i.e., predating entry into college or incidental to the present environment)? The latter kinds of problems can be classified as remedial and require the skills of professional helpers.

3. Are the problems interpersonal or intrapersonal in nature? Problems concerning relationships with peers, teachers, parents, or administrators are most commonly thought of as being developmental, provided there is not a long history of such reoccurring difficulties. However, problems that have persisted for a period of months or years and that are reflected by highly unusual, self-defeating, or self-destructive behavior patterns should be viewed as being remedial and require the expertise of a professional helper.

Trainers can consult Meade (1978) for specific training models in the area of communication skills.

Area V. Setting Goals and Writing Behavioral Objectives: Outcome Objectives

1. *Advisors can assist students in formulating realistic academic, personal and career goals.*

2. *Advisors can assist students in identifying and writing personally meaningful behavioral objectives related to student goals.*

The advisor can make a significant contribution to students' personal, academic and career development by assisting them in the process of establishing goals and objectives. Many students flounder in college because they lack direction. Many are pursuing goals that are more important to other significant people in their lives (parents, spouses, friends, and so on) than to themselves. As a result it becomes very difficult for students to muster their energies to meet others' goals. Academic advisors should be skilled in the process of goal setting. If they can assist students in formulating personal goals and then help them establish behavior objectives to meet these goals, they will be teaching students a skill that can be used not only in college but throughout life. Writers such as Miller and Prince (1976), Ender, McCaffrey and Miller (1979), and DeRisi and Butz (1975) will acquaint the reader with the goal setting area and provide several useful techniques that can be used to teach the content of this area.

Area VI. Formal and Informal
Assessment Techniques: Outcome Objectives

1. *Advisors understand and can accurately interpret to students standardized tests such as SAT, ACT, standardized English and math placement/achievement.*

2. *Advisors can use informal assessment techniques, such as assessment interviews, with students in the process of setting academic and personal goals.*

Much of the dialogue between the advisor and the advisee falls into the realm of assessment. Assessment is the gathering of vital information necessary for making informed and satisfying academic, personal and career decisions. The advisor should have available the results of formal assessments of students prior to and during their enrollment. These data include high school and college grades and grade point averages, standardized test results in academic areas, and interest areas indicated by the student on admission forms or as provided by CEEB or ACT. This formal assessment information should be used along with informal methods for helping students better understand themselves. A systematic means of gathering and recording both informal and formal assessment data, such as using the Student Developmental Profile and Planning Record (Winston, Miller and Prince, 1979a), may be incorporated into the advising program.

The most frequently used informal assessment method is the assessment interview. Advisors need to learn how to conduct an assessment interview (Ender, McCaffrey and Miller, 1979; Cormier and Cormier, 1979) with advisees. This interview follows the format of: opening the interview by establishing rapport, following general leads provided by the student, following up on important leads by asking open-ended questions, pointing out discrepancies that conflict with formal assessment information, and urging the student to clarify options related to academic, personal and career decisions. The ability of advisors to use effective communication skills as they conduct assessment interviews is extremely important and necessary, if the students are to feel comfortable disclosing personal information and concerns. The advisor must understand that the process of assessment is necessary if appropriate goals are to be established by advisees. Both goal setting and assessment are conducted with students' participation and not done to or for them.

Area VII. Decision Making Stragegies:
Outcome Objectives

1. *Advisors understand several simple decision-making models appropriate for student use.*

2. *Advisors can assist students in analyzing their present decision-making strategies and can teach them to use appropriate techniques.*
Students can be aided in making decisions if advisors can teach them several decision-making strategies. The areas of goal setting and assessment previously discussed are part of the decision-making process. It is very helpful when advisors can aid students to structure their decision making processes. One viable decision making procedure follows these steps: (1) helping students clarify and understand their value system; (2) assisting students in determining whether their goals are consistent with their values; (3) asking students to explore and gather all relevant information concerning each alternative decision that can be made in light of its outcomes and stated personal, academic and career goals; (4) making a decision in light of the alternatives and goals discussed; and (5) evaluating the soundness of the decision in terms of actual outcomes (Ender, McCaffrey, and Miller, 1979). Other models and sources which might be useful include Gelatt and others (1973), and Scholz, Prince and Miller (1975). As is true of goal setting and assessment techniques, when advisors teach students decision making strategies it helps develop skills that can be used time and again.

Area VIII. Career Exploration:
Outcome Objectives

1. *Advisors can help students identify academic requirements and skills that are related to specific careers.*
2. *Advisors can teach students to match various majors and career areas.*
Many students are unsuccessful and leave the college environment without a degree because they see no apparent relationship between the curriculum and their personal career and vocational options. This is especially true for those students who take the bulk of their courses in the core curriculum and have not narrowed down or declared a major area of study. The first two years of college for students who are undecided as to their major area of study can be extremely frustrating. Academic advisors can urge students to experiment with elective hours, take courses in possible interest areas, consistent with their academic skill levels. Urging undecided students to visit the career counseling center, to take interest inventories, and to visit academic departments on campus to interview various faculty about career options in different degree programs encourages students to become actively involved in career exploration. Also, helping students understand the significance and importance of the core curriculum as it relates to life skills and a democratic society assists students in understanding the relevance of courses they are presently taking. The previous training areas of communications skills, goal setting, assessment and decision

making all come into play as advisors assist students in career exploration. Readers are urged to consult Gordon (1981) for further elaboration on career choice as it relates to developmental theory and recommendations for academic advising. Other helpful sources include Bolles (1974, 1978).

Area IX. Study Skills and
Time Management: Outcome Objectives

1. *Advisors can teach students simple techniques for making better use of their time, such as setting priorities and making schedules which include study, sleep, recreation and social activities.*

2. *Advisors can teach students rudimentary processes for improving study efficiency, such as notetaking, use of textbooks, and preparation for examinations.*

The academic advisor should be aware that entering students of whatever age have difficulty in managing their time. For the younger student it may be a matter of too much time about which to make decisions and for the older student too little time to get the course work completed. All age groups can benefit from time management instruction and assistance with planning realistic academic schedules congruent with time restraints and skills levels.

Along with time management instruction students can benefit from acquiring or strengthening academic skills such as notetaking, use of textbooks, and exam preparation. These skills are essential for academic success and retention by the college. Readers may wish to consult Carothers (1977) and Shepherd (1979) for specific strategies when training in this area.

Area X. Campus Resources and
Referral Techniques: Outcome Objectives.

1. *Advisors are well acquainted with the college's student services, opportunities for participation in student organizations and groups, academic support services, as well as community services and programs.*

2. *Advisors can refer students to appropriate resources on campus or in the community.*

3. *Advisors can assess student problems and can take appropriate referral action in serious or emergency situations.*

The student-advisee will have many questions and concerns which cannot be adequately dealt with by the advisor. In many instances the responsibility of the advisor is to help students articulate their questions and concerns and then to refer them to the appropriate campus agency or department. It is of vital importance that advisors know the existing helping agencies and departments on campus, the function of these agencies and the personnel who work in them. A referral is best made to a person rather than to a building or office. Advisors should be encouraged to follow-up with advisees to determine the outcome of the visit. Examples of how several universities teach advisors referral skills may be found in Crockett (1978b).

Area XI. Awareness of Special Populations on the College Campus: Outcome Objectives.

1. *Advisors will be aware of the characteristics and needs of special populations of college students seen in the advising process (for instance, returning women, undecided majors, student athletes, handicapped students, veterans, academic high risk students).*

2. *Advisors will develop specific helping strategies which can be used when dealing with the unique needs of various special populations.*

The training components presented to this point cover specific areas of knowledge and helping skills which can be utilized by advisor as they have contact with all student-advisees. However, special populations (see Chapter Five) that exist on today's college campuses have specific needs which should be recognized in the advising process. Training in this area should include the identification of special populations, their unique needs, lifestyles and culture and subsequent helping strategies that can be utilized by advisors as they interact with these individuals.

The Training Program: Trainer Decisions

Readers may find themselves overwhelmed by the comprehensive nature of this proposed training program and decide that it is impossible to include all eleven areas in their training package. Even though we would argue that the eleven components of training described are essential areas of skill and knowledge needed by advisors in institutions truly committed to the concept of developmental advising, we also realize that commitment is often dampened by lack of faculty time for training, limited trainer competencies, inadequate reward systems for participation in the training program and myopic views as to roles of advisors and intent of the advising program.

If those responsible for advisor training programs cannot overcome these restraints, we suggest that a less comprehensive initial program concentrating on many of the basic core helping skills (effective communication, assessment, goal setting, referral techniques and study skills) and most basic knowledge areas (academic policies and registration, career information, developmental theory, campus resources/services, and needs of unique populations) be designed. Long range goals could include expanding the training program to become more comprehensive and intensive. It is our conviction that the quality and rigor of the training program is directly reflected in the quality of academic advising experienced by students. There are no easy answers or short cuts.

Critical Issues in Training Advisors

As Kramer and Gardner (1978) have pointed out, no advising program begins *de novo*. This, however, may not be true of advisor training programs; systematic and indepth training for academic advisors is rare. Because of the often held view that "anyone with a doctorate ought to be able to do something as simple as advising" (Kramer and Gardner, 1978, p. 1.97), training beyond provision of a catalogue, schedule of classes and a registration procedures manual has often been a low priority. A number of issues germane to advisor training need to be addressed if institutions are to offer systematic advisor training programs which have as their intent developmental advising.

Format. Two models for training academic advisors predominate the literature: workshops and continuing inservice (Grites, 1978). The workshop approach may be one or two full days or weekends. Typically these occur shortly before the beginning of the fall term. The inservice sessions typically are periodically scheduled and may be used to either communicate information (such as, changing graduation requirements, class registration procedures) or to help advisors gain or refine skills needed in the advising process. One novel approach suggested by Kramer and Gardner (1978) is individual face-to-face contracting between the "advising manager" (program administrator) and the advisor. They argue that this ensures a clear understanding concerning expectations and avoids two pitfalls often associated with training advisors, namely it avoids labeling "training" as "help for ignorant faculty and staff" and it does not put these individuals in the position where they tacitly acknowledge (even through attendance!) they need help.

We suggest a different model. *Training takes place before selection of academic advisors.* In other words, training would become a prerequisite for selection. Such an approach has several advantages: (1) following training, selection can be based upon criteria relevant to advising since all who have been in training will have been observed in a number of the roles advisors will be expected to fill; (2) advisors will have the skills and competencies needed for their job before they are ever asked to see the first student thereby increasing their confidence and ability to perform in this role; and (3) training prior to selection will clearly communicate several important ideas (for example, specific skills are required to be an effective advisor, the institution clearly values advising and there are right and wrong ways of doing some things).

Such a training program would meet for three hours per week for ten to twelve weeks, probably during the winter or spring prior to implementation of the "new" advising program the following fall. In order for this to work a number of conditions need to exist. Specifically, (1) there must be rewards for participating in training (preferably additional salary or reduced teaching load), (2) academic administrators (vice presidents, deans, department chairpersons) must be openly supportive of a new thrust in academic advising, and (3) key faculty leaders (and in some colleges union leaders) must understand the ideas and give at least tacit approval. It appears obvious that training issues are an integral part of an overall advising program and cannot be viewed in isolation.

Selling the Idea of Training. The most likely approach for selling the idea of training advisors is under the rubric of faculty and staff development, an idea familiar to most faculty members, student development educators and academic administrators. If effective faculty and staff development programs already exist on a campus, the idea of training may be incorporated into existing structures. Francis (1975, p. 720) defines faculty development programs as "an institutional process which seeks to modify the attitudes, skills, and behavior of faculty members toward greater competence and effectiveness in meeting student needs, their own needs, and the needs of the institution. Successful programs change the way faculty feel about their professional roles, and alter the way they carry them out in practice." This is an excellent rationale as one advocates the need for academic advisor training programs. A better description would be difficult to find for formulating the goals of academic advisor training.

Training Techniques. A well conceived, theoretically sound, training plan is essential for a successful training program. However, that alone is not enough. A number of other critical issues such as who leads the training, which forms of instruction should be employed and reward/ incentives for training need to be examined also.

Who should be responsible for training is a critical question, which, if not properly considered, can undermine a training program from its inception. When training faculty members, it is essential that the trainer be someone who has creditability in their eyes. In other words training leaders need credentials similar to faculty members, that is advanced degree (preferably doctorate), academic rank and teaching experience. We suggest that a training team be used. One or two people from the student affairs division (who should possess well developed group leadership skills, experience in teaching interpersonal communications skills, a commitment to quality academic advising, an indepth understanding of student development theories, knowledge and utilization of campus resources, and experience in applying assessment, decision making and goal setting interventions with undergraduate students) could be joined by one or two faculty members or academic administrators. These "faculty types" should bring with them high levels of commitment to quality academic advising and advisor training, experience as an advisor and faculty member, knowledge of the curriculum, and an appreciation of institutional and departmental policies and politics. The presence of a relatively high level academic administrator can signal the approval of academic deans or vice presidents.

It is important that training be, in fact, a team effort, with all members sharing in the planning and assuming responsibility for its success, because anything less will become obvious to the participants very early and can become a negative influence. For this reason all team members should attend each session, with responsibilities for conducting specific units and sessions being shared. The academic-side leaders can perform an important and valuable role model function during training by demonstrating a willingness to take risks, especially during experiential activities, and by sharing their feelings when appropriate. As noted in Chapter One, if quality academic advising is to exist on a campus there must be effective collaboration between the student affairs division and the academic affairs division; this collaboration should be very obvious and visible during the training experience.

The form instruction takes is a crucial issue which should be carefully considered during the planning phase. Faculty members and staff are well-educated, efficient learners who have internalized a particular view of the world, a specific kind of logic, and a preferred means of dealing with people, things, and ideas, often without their being consciously aware of it (Mitroff and Kilmann, 1978). Because the basic assumptions and ways of viewing the world of faculty and staff can be so different, selecting instructional methodologies appropriate for advisor training becomes a critical task. A diversity of backgrounds of those on the training team can help attend to these differences during planning. Special attention should be paid to planned activities which are designed to specifically address the affective dimensions. Some prospective advisors may be uncomfortable during activities which require them to function in a feeling mode, something their style of inquiry may label as undesirable. They may need considerable support and encouragement, and always should be given the option not to participate (without prejudice). However, it is important to note persons who seem to have considerable difficulty because, as Kramer and Gardner (1978) note, advisors who are fearful of their own incompetence tend to project them onto the students with whom they have contact. When this happens, they argue, advisors tend to feel more positive about themselves and more negative about those "incompetent students" with whom they are required to deal. A model which provides training prior to selection would allow for not selecting persons who lack the basic skills for dealing with students' affective concerns.

There must be an incentive or reward system for participation in training. Grites (1978) has suggested that honoraria might be paid where possible. Lacking the resources for that, other alternatives, in descending order of probable effectiveness, include reduced teaching load during training, promise of summer employment, free meals associated with training sessions, or official recognition with letters to department chairpersons and deans. It is important to reward training in currency valued by the participants. To expect committed and enthusiastic participation in training without adequate rewards is to come to bat with two strikes against you. If quality advising is important to the institution, then the institution must communicate this commitment in tangible ways.

Educational institutions that implement training programs as advocated in this chapter are making a commitment to the development of students, faculty and staff. They are recognizing that academic advising is an integral part of the higher education process and not a minor support service only tangentially related to the purpose of the institution.

References

Bolles, R. N. *What Color Is Your Parachute?: A Practical Manual for Job-Hunters and Career Changers.* Berkeley, Calif.: Ten Speed Press, 1974.

Bolles, R. N. *The Three Boxes of Life and How To Get Out of Them: An Introduction to Life/Work Planning.* Berkeley, Calif.: Ten Speed Press, 1978.

Brown, R. D., and Citrin, R. "A Student Development Transcript: Assumptions, Uses and Formats." *Journal of College Student Personnel,* 1977, *18,* 163–168.

Carkhuff, R. R., Pierce, R. M., and Cannon, J. R. *The Art of Helping.* Amherst, Mass.: Human Resource Development Press, 1977.

Carothers, R. L. *Strategy: An Academic Survival Kit.* Dubuque: Kendall/Hunt, 1977.

Chickering, A. W. *Education and Identity.* San Francisco: Jossey-Bass, 1969.

Chickering, A. W., and Havighurst, R. J. "The Life Cycle." In A. W. Chickering and Associates, *The Modern American College: Responding to the New Realities of Diverse Students and a Changing Society.* San Francisco: Jossey-Bass, 1981.

Cormier, W. H., and Cormier, L. S. *Interviewing Strategies for Helpers: A Guide to Assessment, Treatment, and Evaluation.* Monterey, Calif.: Brooks/Cole Publishing, 1979.

Crockett, D. S. "Academic Advising: A Cornerstone of Student Retention." In L. Noel (Ed.), *New Directions for Student Services: Reducing the Dropout Rate,* no. 3. San Francisco: Jossey-Bass, 1978a.

Crockett, D. S. (Ed). *Academic Advising: A Resource Document.* Iowa City: The American College Testing Program, 1978b.

Crookston, B. B. "A Developmental View of Academic Advisement as Teaching." *Journal of College Student Personnel,* 1972, *13*(1), 12–17.

Delworth, U. (Ed.). *New Directions for Student Services: Training Competent Staff,* no. 2. San Francisco: Jossey-Bass, 1978.

Delworth, U., and Aulepp, L. *Training Manual for Paraprofessional and Allied Professional Programs.* Boulder, Colo.: Western Interstate Commission for Higher Education, 1976.

DeRisi, W. J., and Butz, G. *Writing Behavioral Contracts: A Case Simulation Practice Manual.* Champaign, Ill.: Research Press, 1975.

102

Ender, S. C., McCaffrey, S. S., and Miller, T. K. *Students Helping Students: A Training Manual for Peer Helpers on the College Campus.* Athens, Ga.: Student Development Associates, 1979.

Ender, S. C., and McFadden, R. "Training the Student Paraprofessional Helper." In F. B. Newton and K. L. Ender (Eds.), *Student Development Practices: Strategies for Making a Difference.* Springfield, Ill.: Charles C. Thomas, 1980.

Francis, J. B. "How Do We Get There From Here? Program Design for Faculty Development." *Journal of Higher Education,* 1975, *46* (6), 719–732.

Gazda, G. M. and others. *Human Relations Development: A Manual for Educators.* Boston: Allyn and Bacon, 1973.

Gelatt, H. B. and others. *Decisions and Outcomes: A Leader's Guide.* New York: College Entrance Examination Board, 1973.

Gordon, V. N. "The Undecided Student: A Developmental Perspective." *Personnel and Guidance Journal,* 1981, *59* (7), 433–439.

Grites, T. J. "Training the Academic Advisor." In D. S. Crockett (Ed.), *Academic Advising: A Resource Document.* Iowa City, Iowa: American College Testing Program, 1978.

Heath, D. H. *Growing Up in College.* San Francisco: Jossey-Bass, 1968.

Knefelkamp, L. L. (Ed.). *Manual for the Student Activities Involvement Log.* College Park: University of Maryland Office of Campus Activities, 1980.

Kramer, H. C., and Gardner, R. E. "Managing Faculty Advising." In D. S. Crockett (Ed.), *Academic Advising: A Resource Document.* Iowa City: American College Testing Program, 1978.

Levinson, D. J., and others. *The Seasons of a Man's Life.* New York: Knopf, 1978.

McCaffrey, S. S., and Miller, T. K. "Mentoring: An Approach to Academic Advising," In F. B. Newton and K. L. Ender (Eds.), *Student Development Practices: Strategies for Making a Difference.* Springfield, Ill.: Charles C. Thomas, 1980.

Meade, C. J. "Interpersonal Skills: Who, What, When, Why." In U. Delworth (Ed.), *New Directions for Student Services: Training Competent Staff,* no. 2. San Francisco: Jossey-Bass, 1978.

Miller, T. K., and Prince, J. S. *The Future of Student Affairs: A Guide to Student Development for Tomorrow's Higher Education.* San Francisco: Jossey-Bass, 1976.

Mitroff, I. I., and Kilmann, R. H. *Methodological Approaches to Social Science.* San Francisco: Jossey-Bass, 1978.

Perry, W., Jr. *Intellectual and Ethical Development in the College Years.* New York: Holt, Rinehart & Winston, 1970.

Scholz, N. T., Prince, J. S., and Miller, G. P. *How to Decide: A Guide for Women.* New York: College Entrance Examination Board, 1975.

Shepherd, J. F. *College Study Skills.* Boston: Houghton Mifflin Company, 1979.

Winston, R. B., Jr., Miller, T. K., and Prince, J. S. *Assessing Student Development: A Preliminary Manual for the Student Developmental Task Inventory (Revised, Second Edition) and the Student Developmental Profile and Planning Record.* Athens, Ga.: Student Development Associates, 1979a.

Winston, R. B., Jr., Miller, T. K., and Prince, J. S. *Student Developmental Task Inventory.* Athens, Ga.: Student Development Associates, 1979b.

Steven C. Ender is assistant professor in the department of counseling and human development services at the University of Georgia.

Roger B. Winston, Jr. is assistant professor in the student personnel in Higher Education Program and Director of the Student Development Laboratory at the University of Georgia Department of Counseling and Human Development Services. He has helped lead workshops and been a consultant on training peer helpers and professional staff development.

A brief introduction to the literature on academic advising is presented.

Academic Advising Resources: A Sampling

Roger B. Winston, Jr.

During the past ten years there has been an explosion of interest in and concern about academic advising. National conferences on academic advising began to be held in the late 1970s; the American College Testing Program began to hold regional workshops/seminars to capacity audiences at about the same time. One result was the creation of the National Academic Advising Association, which now holds an annual conference. It has also begun to publish a journal (*NACADA Journal,* edited by Edward L. Jones, University of Washington, Box 36, Seattle, Washington 98195), with its first issue in January 1981.

This brief bibliography is intended to serve as an introduction for those readers who are new to the area by providing a cross section of the literature including theoretical conceptualizations, research concerning comparative effectiveness, and practical resources.

Biggs, D. A., Brodie, J. S., and Barnhart, W. J. "The Dynamics of Undergraduate Academic Advising." *Research in Higher Education,* 1975, *3,* 345-357.

    Based on survey data from faculty at five colleges, the work of the advisor was classified as dealing with (1) special academic, social or financial problems; (2) emotional or psychological problems; (3) academic and

R. Winston, S. Ender, T. Miller (Eds.). *New Directions for Student Services: Developmental Approaches to Academic Advising,* no. 17. San Francisco: Jossey-Bass, March 1982.

career guidance problems, and (4) administrative activities. Most advisors spent more time in administrative activities than in the other categories and reported feeling it inappropriate for them to deal with personal or social problems.

Brown, C. R., and Myers, R. "Student *vs.* Faculty Curriculum Advising." *Journal of College Student Personnel,* 1975, *16,* 226–231.

Advisee perceptions of faculty advisors were compared with those of student (peer) advisors. Advisees perceived peer advisors more positively than their faculty counterparts. Peer advisors were seen as treating the advising process as a joint decision making process, while faculty advisors were perceived as either making decisions for advisees or leaving the decision up to them alone.

Crockett, D. S. (Ed.). *Academic Advising: A Resource Document.* Iowa City: The American College Testing Program, 1978 (and supplement, 1979).

These two loose-leaf binder collections of materials are an invaluable resource for anyone seeking to establish or maintain an effective advising program. They contain invited essays by leaders in the advising field, as well as other materials, such as descriptions of models presently in use, excerpts from handbooks, training materials, journal articles, and annotated bibliographies. Subjects covered include confidentiality, evaluation instruments, training tips, handbooks, minority students and many more.

Crookston, B. B. "A Developmental View of Academic Advising as Teaching." *Journal of College Student Personnel,* 1972, *13,* 12–17.

The difference between developmental and prescriptive advising is delineated. Crookston advocates developmental advising which is based on the nature and quality of the relationship between student and advisor. Advising is viewed as a teaching function characterized by a negotiated contract concerning expectations and responsibilities.

Grites, T. J. *Academic Advising: Getting Us Through the Eighties.* Washington, D.C.: AAHE-ERIC Higher Education Research Report, No. 7, 1979.

This research report presents an excellent comprehensive review and synthesis of the literature on academic advising. It traces its historical development to current models and practices. A variety of delivery systems including faculty advising, advisement centers, peer/paraprofessional advising, computer-assisted advising, group advising, and others are described.

Habley, W. R. "Academic Advisement: The Critical Link in Student Retention." *NASPA Journal,* 1981, *18* (4), 45-50.

The author argues that academic advising has a direct and critical influence on a college's retention of students. Viewed from a retention perspective, academic advising is seen as a means of providing assistance to students in mediating the dissonance between their expectations and the realities of the educational environment.

Johnson, C. W., and Pinkney, J. W. "Outreach: Counseling Service Impacts on Faculty Advising of Students." *Journal of College Student Personnel,* 1980, *21,* 80-84.

A counseling center offered faculty advisors short-term workshops that focused on the definition of the advisor-advisee relationship, communication skills, and goal setting techniques. Six months later workshop participants reported making substantial changes in their advising practice, but the control group reported making few changes.

Kramer, H. C., and Gardner, R. E. *Advising by Faculty.* Washington, D.C.: National Education Association, 1977.

This monograph examines in some detail the goals of academic advising, assumptions about students and their growth, and the nature of an effective advising process. Critical to effective advising is building and maintaining a relationship between advisor and student and using the role modeling process.

Mash, D. J. "Academic Advising: Too Often Taken for Granted." *College Board Review,* 1978, *107,* 32-36.

A developmental approach to academic advising is proposed which would include planning, evaluating and reevaluating advising programs in light of the individual goals of students, their backgrounds, expectations, academic deficiencies, and academic strengths.

Moore, K. M. "Faculty Advising: Panacea or Placebo?" *Journal of College Student Personnel,* 1976, *12,* 371-375.

Through a survey of students and faculty, Moore sought to determine the amount and nature of student-faculty contact in the advising process. Registration was the most frequent topic of discussion followed by graduation requirements. It was concluded that faculty have little involvement with students' personal growth, especially if counseling related skills are needed.

Polson, C. J., and Cashin, W. E. "Research Priorities for Academic Advising: Results of Survey of NACADA Membership." *NACADA Journal,* 1981, *1* (1), 34-43.

The most frequently identified problems needing research included: (1) overall impact of academic advising on students' lives, (2) effectiveness of programs designed to serve special student populations, (3) kinds of advisors who are most effective, that is, faculty, professional counselors, professional advisors, peer advisors, (4) effectiveness of various delivery systems, and (5) relationship between advising and retention.

Roger B. Winston, Jr., is assistant professor in the Department of Counseling and Human Development Services at the University of Georgia. His research interests include graduate students and their environments, assessment of college student growth and development, and student affairs organizations and service delivery.

Index

A

Abel, J., 55, 64

Academic advising: administration role in, 10–11, 22, 41; antecedent conditions for, 15; application of theories in, 24-28; assignment to, 61; and campus and community resources, 8; characteristics of, 7–8; as collaboration, 8, 10–12; and commitment to relativism, 33-35; commitment to, levels of, 57–58; content of, 61; decisions about, 58–59; delivery systems for, 39–53; developmental, defined, 8; developmental, rationale for, 4–6, 20–28; developmental, transition to, 68; developmental model of, 21–23; developmental principles for, 20-21; direct approach to, 79–80; and dualism, 28–29; evaluation of, 55–66; expectations about, 58; faculty role in, 11, 43–44; as goal related, 7; goals of, 58; in groups, 47, 76–77; and human growth, 7; human relationship in, 7; and institutional politics, 13; intrusive approach to, 70; literature on, 85–88; and multiplicity, 29–31; and organizational norms, 13–14; potential of, 1; as process, 7, 61; professional advisor role in, 11–12, 44–45; rationale for, 4–6, 20–28; redefinition of, 6–8; and relativism, 31–33; research on, 5–6; resources for, 62; and responsiveness to change, 15; and reward system, 14; scheduling of, 61; SPICE and Perry scheme for, 24-35; strategies for, 70–72, 73–75, 76–77, 78–79; as student development, 3–18; student development theory as foundation for, 19–37; for subpopulations, 67–83; task analysis of, 59–60

Accrediting associations, and athletes, 78–79

Administrators, role of, 10–11, 22, 41

Adult students: characteristics of, 69–70; and classroom experiences, 71; and credit by alternative means, 71; programs for, 72–73; resources for, 71–72; strategies for, 70–72; as subpopulation 69–73

Advisement centers, role of, 48–49

Advising. See Academic advising

Advisors: attitudes of, 61; and commitment in relativism, 35; and dualism, 29; evaluation of, 61; institutional responsibilities of, 8–9; load of, 43, 70; as models, 7, 9–10, 11, 24; and multiplicity, 30, 31; paraprofessional, 46; peer, 45–46, 77; professional, 11–12, 14, 44–45; and relativism, 32–33; responsibilities of, 8–10; selection of, 61; skills of, 61; and students, 9–10; training of, 9, 22, 62

Allegheny County, Community College of, adult students at, 72

Allport, G. W., 34, 36

American College Testing Program, 62, 85

Ancheta, B., 69, 81

Anderson, D., 45, 52

Andrews, P., 45, 52

Astin, A. W., 3, 5, 11, 16, 55, 64

Athletes: alternative career planning for, 79; characteristics of, 77–78; programs for, 80; strategies for, 78–79; as subpopulation, 77–80

Atkins, C. E., 47, 50

Austin, A. D., 77, 82

B

Baldwin, R. A., 45, 51

Ball State University, advisement center at, 48

Bargeron, A., 2

Barman, C. R., 46, 51

Barnhart, W. J., 85–86

Barr, M. J., 13, 14, 16

Barry College, high-risk students at, 75